DATE DUE

# Nat Love

# Legends of the Wild West

Sitting Bull

Billy the Kid

Calamity Jane

Buffalo Bill Cody

Crazy Horse

Davy Crockett

Wyatt Earp

Geronimo

Wild Bill Hickok

Jesse James

Nat Love

Annie Oakley

# Legends of the Wild West

# Nat Love

Barbara Lee Bloom

CHELSEA HOUSE
PUBLISHERS
An imprint of Infobase Publishing

**Nat Love**

Copyright © 2010 by Infobase Publishing

Chelsea House
An imprint of Infobase Publishing
132 West 31st Street
New York NY 10001

**Library of Congress Cataloging-in-Publication Data**
Bloom, Barbara Lee, 1943-
  Nat Love / by Barbara Lee Bloom.
    p. cm. — (Legends of the wild West)
  Includes bibliographical references and index.
  ISBN 978-1-60413-599-2 (hardcover)
  1.  Love, Nat, 1854-1921—Juvenile literature. 2.  African American cowboys—West (U.S.)—Biography—Juvenile literature. 3.  Cowboys—West (U.S.)—Biography—Juvenile literature. 4.  West (U.S.)—Biography—Juvenile literature. I. Title. II. Series.
  F594.L892B56 2010
  978'.00496073'009—dc22
  [B]                            2009034814

Chelsea House books are available at special discounts when purchased in bulk quantities for businesses, associations, institutions, or sales promotions. Please call our Special Sales Department in New York at (212) 967-8800 or (800) 322-8755.

You can find Chelsea House on the World Wide Web at
http://www.chelseahouse.com

Text design by Kerry Casey
Cover design by Keith Trego
Composition by Kerry Casey
Cover printed by Bang Printing, Brainerd, Minn.
Book printed and bound by Bang Printing, Brainerd, Minn.
Date printed: January, 2010
Printed in the United States of America

10 9 8 7 6 5 4 3 2 1

This book is printed on acid-free paper.

All links and Web addresses were checked and verified to be correct at the time of publication. Because of the dynamic nature of the Web, some addresses and links may have changed since publication and may no longer be valid.

# CONTENTS

# "AN UNUSUALLY ADVENTUROUS LIFE"

Nat (pronounced Nate) Love and 11 other strong cowboys, 5 of them also black like Love, lined up on horseback on July 4, 1876, in Deadwood, South Dakota. It was the end of a long cattle drive and all the cowpunchers gathered to celebrate an uproarious Fourth in typical cowboy fashion. They were holding a contest to see which of them could rope, tie, bridle, saddle, and stay on to ride a wild horse in the shortest time. Each cowboy was assigned a different mustang, and each sat on his own pony awaiting the signal.

When the gunshot echoed across the prairie, Love spurred his pony racing toward his mustang, rope in hand. Quickly he whirled his lariat in the air and looped it over the head of the wild horse. As the horse struggled to break free, Love tightened the rope. He jumped from his pony, and held the wild one, slipping a bridle over its head. Still holding the mustang, he tossed a saddle over the back of the twisting, turning horse and cinched it, before he swung up to ride. Love later said in his autobiography, *The Life and Adventures of Nat Love*, "I never had a horse pitch with me so much as that mustang, but I never stopped sticking my spurs into and using my quirt [rawhide whip] on his flanks until I proved his master." Despite the kicking and bucking of his wild mustang, Love got on and rode the horse in just nine minutes. He was the first to complete the job. The second cowboy finished more than three minutes later. As the dust settled, Love was pronounced the winner and awarded a $200 prize. More important, the crowd of cowboys gave him the name "Deadwood Dick," and declared him the champion roper of the western cattle country.

That day, Deadwood Dick was the hero of the town and all the cowboys who had just finished a tough cattle drive. In the saloons and dance halls like the Bell Union Saloon and the Nattal & Mann's #10, the cowboys danced, drank, shouted, and gambled for several days, helped along by Love's prize money. Love proudly bore the name Deadwood Dick for the rest of his life on the range. As a young boy, though, Love could only dream about such an accomplishment, for he started life as a slave.

## BORN INTO SLAVERY

Nat Love was born on a Tennessee plantation in June 1854. The exact date is unknown because slave babies were considered unimportant so their birthdays were not noted. Like most slaves, Love took the last name of his master and owner, Robert Love, who owned both his mother and father. His mother and father had no control over his young life; instead, it was Master Love, who owned many slaves and a huge plantation near Nashville. Those born into slavery did not have birthdays, or last names, or families to call their own. If the slave owner wanted to sell a slave baby or its mother or father, he was within his rights; slaves had no legal rights.

Slavery was a system that had existed in the United States for 168 years before the drafting of the Constitution in 1788. Although many Northern states soon outlawed it, Southern states continued to allow slavery because it was such a profitable system.

In 1793, Eli Whitney invented the cotton gin (short for cotton engine). This machine quickly separated the cotton fibers from the seeds, a job that required considerable labor when done by hand. The gin caused massive growth in the production of cotton, which

Slavery in Colonial America began with the arrival of the Dutch ship the *White Lion* in 1619, which had onboard 20 Angolan slaves. By 1860, out of a total population of 31.4 million in the country, nearly 4 million were slaves.

resulted in the expanded use of slaves to plant and harvest the cotton. Slaveholders tried to justify the practice by saying it was their duty to take care of an "inferior race." In addition, the Bible used the term *servant*, and so Southern slaveholders often said it was "the will of God to hold slaves." By the time Love was born, most people in the North had come to see the evils of the system. People who worked to rid the country of this horrid institution became known as abolitionists because they wanted to abolish slavery.

Slaves' daily lives were filled with hard work and poverty, and their toil provided the slave states with labor to grow cotton, tobacco, indigo, and food crops. African-American men held in bondage built roads, houses, cities, ships, and bridges. African-American men, women, and children labored so others could prosper and sell the goods they produced. Despite having nothing more than the clothes on their backs and whatever food that was given to them, slaves had to obey their master or mistress. In the master-slave relationship, the slaveholder set the rules for daily life. While some masters treated their slaves with a measure of kindness, most believed as one plantation owner said in *A People and a Nation*, "[S]laves can't be governed except by the whip." A slave was considered chattel, like a cow or horse, which could be beaten or sold at will. Henry Louis Gates recounts in *The Classic Slave Narratives* the words of Mary Prince, a slave woman, "Slavery hardens white people's hearts toward the blacks…." She explained that her mistress beat her with "her own cruel hand….To strip me naked to hang me up by the wrists and lay my flesh open with the cow-skin, was an ordinary punishment for even a slight offense."

To survive under such conditions meant that slaves had to learn to endure and adjust. Some found it unbearable and tried to escape. Those who succeeded made it to the open territories of the West or up north into Canada. Historians estimate that about 60,000 slaves escaped to freedom, and those who remained behind longed to be free. As Prince wrote, "All slaves want to be free—to be free is very sweet…. The man that says slaves [are] quite happy in slavery—that they don't want to be free—that man is either ignorant or a lying person."

## Yearning to Be Free

The anti-slavery North and the slave-owning South were in constant conflict over the institution of slavery. Disagreements over the morality of owning another person and the economic advantages of free labor versus slave plantations brought the conflict to a boil in the late 1850s. Eventually, 11 Southern states seceded, or withdrew, from the United States and formed the Confederate States of

America, creating its own constitution and building its own White House. Twenty-three states remained loyal to the Union, and the nation went to war in 1861. The American Civil War, also called the War Between the States, was fought between the Union and the Confederacy until 1865.

Although the winning of the war by the Union and the Thirteenth Amendment to the U.S. Constitution ended slavery, racial prejudice continued to fester in most Southern states. Despite the Fourteenth and Fifteenth Amendments giving all men equal rights and voting privileges, by the early 1900s African Americans in the South had lost their civil rights. They were forced to use segregated public facilities, sit in separate compartments on trains and trolleys, and refused service in restaurants, hotels, and any public places where whites wanted to exclude them. Most Southern states found ways to deny them the right to vote. All this was done both legally and illegally. Laws that reinforced these limits became known as Jim Crow laws. The U.S. Supreme Court struck down the Civil Rights Act of 1875, which outlawed segregation, and in 1896 it decided in a case called *Plessey v. Ferguson* that "separate but equal" public facilities were legal. The public facilities for colored people (which was what African Americans were called at that time), such as schools, were kept separate, but they were inferior, not equal.

Once he was no longer a slave, Nat Love wanted to flee the degrading conditions of life as an African American in the South. He yearned for real freedom, so he left the Old South to seek an education and to escape poverty and prejudice. What he found in the Wild West was a life of hard physical labor and danger, but he was less limited by racial discrimination and segregation, except in the occasional dance hall or saloon. In the rugged life of a cowboy, a man was more often judged by his cowpunching skills (keeping control over a herd of cattle) than by the color of his skin. When the Western frontier faded as railroads, towns, and cities grew and owners of huge cattle ranches built fences to keep in their cattle, Love left the cowboy life and became a Pullman porter on the luxury passenger trains. Though white cowboys with Love's talent often became engineers, managers, or conductors on the railroads, the only job

Booker T. Washington was a former slave who was freed in 1865, at the end of the Civil War. Washington believed that African Americans should concentrate not on fighting for civil rights and the vote but on accumulating wealth and getting an industrial education. Blacks in the North, like W.E.B. Du Bois, disagreed with these priorities and thought Washington was too accommodating to white interests.

open to an African American was as a porter. A porter's job was to serve the passengers, carrying their bags, polishing their shoes, bringing them newspapers, and in many ways performing the job of a servant. Most African Americans like Love had no choice but to accept their second-class role in this country until the civil rights movement of the 1950s and 1960s began to bring changes. In 1905, Love left his job as a Pullman porter and headed west to settle in Los Angeles. In those days in that place, he found less segregation and narrow-mindedness. Writing about his life years later, Love never admitted he had faced racial bigotry, and he never complained. Nonetheless, he was a victim of his skin color.

## LOOKING FOR A PLACE IN AMERICAN SOCIETY

A number of African American leaders of Love's era, such as ex-slave Booker T. Washington, were concerned about the place of blacks in mainstream American society. After the Civil War, when Washington became free, he sought an education. As he wrote in his book, *Up from Slavery*, he graduated from college and began a lifelong attempt to raise "his people in their own eyes and those of white Americans." Unfortunately, most white Americans, even those in the North who had opposed slavery, believed African Americans were inferior. In order to give blacks the opportunity for education and advancement, Washington said blacks and whites should segregate, or live and work apart, for their common good. Instead of fighting for political rights, African Americans should work hard and "keep in mind that we shall prosper in proportion as we learn to dignify and glorify common labor," said Washington in his book. With skills and self-help, "the Negro should acquire property."

In 1881, Washington founded Tuskegee Institute in Alabama to teach practical skills to blacks. Many African Americans agreed with Washington on segregation and left the South to set up black communities in Wisconsin, Oklahoma Territory, Kansas, and other places in the western United States. For many years, Washington was considered the spokesman for "his people."

One of Washington's strongest critics was W.E.B. Du Bois, a born freeman who received a Ph.D. from Harvard University in

1895. In his book *The Souls of Black Folk*, Du Bois criticized Washington, saying, "The way for a people to gain their reasonable rights is not by voluntarily throwing them away." Instead, he said, they should attempt to get all the rights of citizenship. Washington's ideas, Du Bois continued, "practically accepted the alleged inferiority of the Negro." In 1909, Du Bois, along with other progressive blacks and whites, formed the National Association for the Advancement of Colored People (NAACP) to end discrimination and segregation and to gain voting rights for blacks. In addition to attempting to bring equality to blacks, Du Bois gave voice to many African-Americans' feelings about fitting into American society. He wrote: "one [an African American] ever feels his twoness—an American, a Negro, two thoughts, two unreconciled strivings, two warring ideals in one dark body."

Whatever a black person felt about his or her place in American society after the Civil War, it was certain he or she faced intolerance and, often, violence. Since Love wrote little about his feelings, except for his horror of slavery, it is difficult to know exactly what they were. In his autobiography, he praised the United States for its beauty and opportunity, but he never suggested he lived life at a disadvantage. As a person who started life as a slave, perhaps the opportunities he found were so much greater than he could ever have imagined as a child that he felt great satisfaction in all he accomplished and experienced. In the West as a cowboy and later as a porter, he found work that paid him a regular wage and allowed him to live with pride.

## THE BLACK COWBOY

In his autobiography, when Love described his life out West, he used humor and exaggeration, which was typical in most cowboy tales of that era. He assured his readers that the book was "a true history of slavery days, life on the great cattle ranges and the plains of the 'wild and wooly' west, based on facts and personal experiences...." Although many cowboys of the early cattle drives wrote

BEADLE'S HALF DIME Library

Copyrighted in 1877, by Beadle and Adams.

Vol. I.  Single Number.  BEADLE AND ADAMS, PUBLISHERS, No. 98 WILLIAM STREET, NEW YORK.  Price, 5 Cents.  No. 1

## Deadwood Dick,

### THE PRINCE OF THE ROAD;

#### OR,

#### THE BLACK RIDER of the BLACK HILLS.

BY EDWARD L. WHEELER.

#### CHAPTER I.

#### FEARLESS FRANK TO THE RESCUE.

On the plains, midway between Cheyenne and the Black Hills, a train had halted for a noonday feed. Not a railway train, mind you, but a line of those white-covered vehicles drawn by strong-limbed mules, which are most properly styled "prairie schooners."

There were four wagons of this type, and they had been drawn in a circle about a camp-fire, over which was roasting a savory haunch of venison. Around the camp-fire were grouped half a score of men, all rough, bearded, and grizzled, with one exception. This being a youth whose age one could have safely put at twenty, so perfectly developed of physique and intelligent of facial appearance was he. There was something about him that was not handsome, and yet you would have been puzzled to tell what it was for his countenance was strikingly handsome, and surely no forte in the crowd was more noticeable for its grace, symmetry, and proportionate development. It would have taken a scholar to have studied out the secret.

He was of about medium stature, and as straight and square-shouldered as an athlete. His complexion was nut-brown, from long exposure to the sun; hair of hue of the raven's wing, and hanging in long, straight strands adown his back; eyes black and piercing as an eagle's; features well molded, with a firm, resolute mouth and prominent chin. He was an interesting specimen of young, healthy manhood, and, even though a youth in years, was one that could command respect, if not admiration, wheresoever he might choose to go.

One remarkable item about his personal appearance, apt to strike the beholder as being exceedingly strange and eccentric, was his costume—buckskin throughout, and that dyed to the brightest scarlet hue.

On being asked the cause of his odd freak of dress, when he had joined the train a few miles out from Cheyenne, the youth had laughingly replied:

"Why, you see, it is to attract buffers, if we should meet any, out on the plains 'twixt this and the Hills."

He gave his name as Fearless Frank, and said he was aiming for the Hills; that if the party in question would furnish him a place among them, he would extend to them his assistance as a hunter, guide, or whatever, until the destination was reached.

Seeing that he was well armed, and judging from external appearances that he would prove a valuable accessory, the miners were nothing loth in accepting his services.

Of the others grouped about the camp-fire only one is specially noticeable, for, as Mark Twain remarks, "the average of gold-diggers look alike." This person was a little, deformed old man; humpbacked, bow-legged, and white-haired, with cross eyes, a large mouth, a big head, set upon a slim, crane-like neck; blue eyes, and an immense brown beard, that flowed downward half-way to the belt about his waist, which contained a small arsenal of knives and revolvers. He hobbled about with a heavy crutch constantly under his left arm, and was certainly a pitiable sight to behold.

He too had joined the caravan after it had quitted Cheyenne, his advent taking place about an hour subsequent to that of Fearless Frank. His name he asserted was Nix—Geoffrey Walsingham Nix—and where he came from, and what he sought in the Black Hills, was simply a matter of conjecture among the miners, as he refused to talk on the subject of his past, present or future.

The train was under the command of an irascible old plainsman who had served out his apprenticeship in the Kansas border war, and whose name was Charity Joe, which, considering his avaricious disposition, was the wrong handle on the wrong man. Charity was the least of all old Joe's redeeming characteristics; charity was the very thing he did not recognize, yet some wag had facetiously branded him Charity Joe, and the appellation had clung to him ever since. He was well advanced in years, yet withal a good trailer and an expert guide, as the success of his many late expeditions into the Black Hills had evidenced.

Those who had heard of Joe's skill as a guide, to trusted themselves in his care, for, while the stages were stopped more or less on each trip, Charity Joe's train invariably went through all safe and sound. This was partly owing to his acquaintance with various bands of Indians, who were the chief cause of annoyance on the trip.

So far we see the train toward the land of gold, without their having seen sight or sound of hostile red-skins, and Charity is just chuckling over his usual good luck.

"I tell ye what, fellers, we've hed a fa'r sort uv a shake, o' car, an' no mistake bout it. Barrin' thar ain't no Sittin' Bulls layin' in wait fer us, behead yander, in thar mounts, I'm o' ther candid opinion we'll get through wi'out scrapin' a ha'r."

"I hope so," said Fearless Frank, rolling over on the grass and gazing at the guide, thoughtfully, "but I doubt it. It seems to me that our bears of mere butchering, lately, than there was a month ago—all on account of the influx of ruffianly characters into the Black Hills."

"Not all owing to that, chip—" interposed "General" Nix, as he had immediately been christened by the miners—"not all owing to that. Thar's them got danged reppur-colored guests uv ther government—they're kickin' up three pints uv they're ruction, more or less—consider'bly more of more than more o' less. Take a passel ov them bar tar-ifies an' shet 'em up inter a prison for three or thirteen yeers, an' ye'd see w'at an impression ed'd make, now. Thar'd be sev'ral less messy-creen a week, an' ye wouldn't see a rufyan one't a month. W'y, gentlefellows, thar'd nev' ver ben a ruffian, ef et hedn't been fer ther cussed Injun tribe—not one! Ther infarnal critters ar' ther instigators uv more deviltry nor a cat wi' nine tails."

"Yes, we will admit that the reds are not of saintly origin," said Fearless Frank, with a quiet smile. "In fact I know of several who are far from being angels, myself. There is old Sitting Bull, for instance, and Lone Lion, Rain-in-the-Face, and Horse with-the-Red-Eye, and so forth, and so forth!"

"Exactly. Every one o' 'em's a danged descendant o' ther old Satan, hisself."

"Layin' aside ther Injun subjeck," said Charity Joe, forking into the roasted venison, "I move thet we take up a silent debate on ther...

Ha! ha! ha! isn't that rich, now?  Ha! ha! ha! arrest Deadwood Dick if you can!

Deadwood Dick was a character that first became popular in dime novels published by Edward Wheeler. The name was so popular, it was used by several men who lived at that time, including Nat Love. Pictured is a page from the first Deadwood Dick series, out of 64 novels published from 1877 to 1897.

autobiographies, Love's is the only one written by a cowboy who was an ex-slave. By the time Love published his book in 1907, a reading public had already delighted in popular "dime-novel" Westerns where cowboys performed heroic deeds. In fact, one of the most popular fiction series, written by Edward L. Wheeler, told about an outlaw hero named Deadwood Dick. This hero is always dressed in black, with a black horse, gloved hands, and a black veil covering his face. Love claimed he was the model for Wheeler's series, although eight other cowboys made the same claim. But just as in all dime-novel Westerns, the hero, Deadwood Dick, is white. Even the old Western films of later years failed to include black cowboys despite there being many of them. Historians writing before the 1960s about the West and the frontier overlooked the roles played by African Americans; today, historians believe about 25 to 30 percent of all cowpunchers were black.

Love, like so many other African Americans, attempted to break away from the poverty, bigotry, and lack of opportunity in the South. Still in his teens, he bravely set off alone to try his luck on the untamed frontier. The Wild West that Love discovered captured the imagination of many Americans and has held it over the years. The cowboy remains one of the most popular images of the American past. And for ex-slave Nat Love, work as a cowboy brought "an unusually adventurous life."

# LIFE AS A SLAVE

Nat's birth, in an old slave cabin on a plantation near Nashville, was noted a few days later in the master's account book as an increase in his property. The Love plantation was in the middle of a belt of plantations where many thousands of slaves were forced to work to make profits for their masters. Slaves performed different types of work on the plantation, and in this world, Nat was born into a privileged position. His mother (who's name is unknown) ran the master's kitchen, which meant she was spared from the heavy labor of working in the fields. His father, Sampson, was foreman over the other slaves, so Sampson, too, held a favored position in the plantation's hierarchy. Nat had a sister, Sally, eight years older, and a brother, Jordan, five years older. Nat's mother had so many chores to do, such as milking the cows and churning the milk into butter, that she had little time to look after her children. Sally helped her mother and shooed flies from the master's table during meals. Young Nat had little supervision, so he learned to be independent and to entertain himself.

Before he could walk, he started pushing a chair around Master Love's dining room table, begging for food like a pet dog. As he grew older, he and Jordan sneaked into the plantation garden and helped themselves to watermelon, sweet potatoes, grapes, corn, and other vegetables. With his good diet, he grew strong and agile. Like

Nat Love's mother was a house slave, meaning a slave who lived and worked inside the master's home. Daily chores included caring for the master's children, serving meals, cooking, and cleaning. Although house slaves were given better food and hand-me-down clothes and had better living quarters than field slaves, house slaves were rarely given a day off from work.

other slave children, Nat discovered how to be creative and flexible. Adults also developed special techniques for surviving in bondage.

## LIFE ON THE PLANTATION

Nat told a story in his autobiography about a day when the master's family went away, and his mother made some wine. Her children, Nat, Sally, and Jordan, watched her press the grapes. They thought the drink looked delicious. She placed the juice in a jug and went about her other work. The children wondered where she would put the sweet drink and planned to find out. Nat and Sally left to rake the vineyards, and Jordan went outside to the hayloft. From there, he watched as his mother left the house. She carried the jug into the garden, but she came out empty-handed. The tall plants had blocked Jordan's view, and he never saw where she hid the jug.

Several days later Nat, Jordan, and Sally walked through the garden sampling vegetables, when they came upon the jug. They dragged it into the cornfield, where they were safe from all eyes, opened it, and sipped the fermented juice, which had turned to wine. It tasted delicious and all three drank their fill before they passed out. By nightfall, their mother grew worried about them, and after calling and looking for them, she took the tracking dogs to search. The dogs led her to the corn patch where she found her three children lying by the empty jug. She was angry. She picked up young Nat and took him to their cabin, but left Sally and Jordan to sleep outside all night. Nat was feverish and sick the next day, as were his brother and sister, but their mother still thrashed them soundly.

Each slave on a plantation worked long hours whether in the master's house cleaning and cooking or in the fields. When the master and his family went to bed, the house slaves were usually finished with their work for the day. The field hands worked from sun up to sun down. They plowed, planted, weeded, and picked the crops. After working in the fields all day, they often had night chores such as cleaning the seeds from the cotton. When Nat was old enough, he helped his mother, sister, and brother weeding the garden, raking the barn and barnyard, feeding the pigs, chickens, horses, dogs, and cows, or any chores he was told to do. On the Love plantation, Sunday was a day of rest for the field hands and children.

Life on the plantation changed little from the cold days of winter to the hot days of summer. Some of the chores changed with the seasons, but there was always work to be done. Besides her duties in the kitchen, Nat's mother wove cloth, which was rough and plain. From it she sewed long cotton shirts for all the slave children. In the winter, the slave children wore only these shirts, and in the summer heat they often went naked. Sometimes in the winter, slaves were given crude leather shoes, but most often they went barefoot. In Nat's family cabin there was a big fireplace and on cold winter nights a small fire they might build. His daily life was one of hard work and poverty, and young Nat also felt deeply the brutality of slavery. As he later wrote in his autobiography:

> I have seen the long cruel lash curl around the shoulders of women who refused to comply with the licentious wishes of the men who owned them.... I have seen the snake-like lash draw blood from the tender limbs of mere babies, hardly more than able to toddle, their only offense being that their skin was black. And young as I was my blood often boiled as I witnessed these cruel sights, knowing that they were allowed by the laws of the land in which I was born.

Although Nat once said his master was kinder than most, in Tennessee and other slave states slaves were sold as chattel on the auction block. Nat believed this was the worst act of slavery. He saw husbands taken from their wives to be sold far away and nursing babies sold to new owners. "Of all the curses of this fair land," Nat said when he had grown up, "the greatest curse of all was the slave auction block of the south, where human flesh was bought and sold."

The laws of the Southern states outlawed the teaching of reading and writing to slaves. Many slaves, though, like Nat's father, found ways to learn to read and to write. Nat's father made him and Jordan practice their letters and taught them to read.

On Sundays, Nat, Jordan, and the neighborhood boys often used their day off to organize rabbit hunts. They would gather up the tracking dogs and follow them through the woods and bramble, chasing a cottontail. The game was rough as they scrambled over stones, brushed up against thorns, or tramped through puddles, but Nat and his friends paid little attention to scratches or blood on their legs or arms. It was common in those days for white and black children to play together when they were young. Sometimes a favorite black playmate became a personal slave to an older white child.

## THE CIVIL WAR

In April 1861, when Nat was almost seven years old, the Civil War began. The slave owners were constantly talking about the Union

# Frederick Douglass

Frederick Douglass had long held a dream—to escape slavery. He had tried once, but was caught and severely punished. Still, he couldn't deny his desire to be free. There were freed African Americans living in the South, and that gave him an idea. At the age of 20, on a September morning in 1838, dressed as a sailor and carrying the proper papers of a friend who was a freed black seaman, he boarded a train in Havre de Grace, Maryland. Douglass knew that if he was caught this time he might never find another chance to be free. Luckily, he reached New York the next day. In the city, he worried about being captured and sent back. He traveled on to Massachusetts where he got work in the shipyards. He spent the rest of his life as a free man and eventually became a famous abolitionist.

In Massachusetts, Douglass attended meetings of the Anti-Slavery Society, and at one, he was asked to tell his story. His speech describing the evils of slavery so moved his audience that he was asked to become a paid lecturer for the society. From this time on, he devoted his life to speaking and writing about abolition and equality for all people. He published his own newspaper *The North Star,* having taught himself to read and write when he was a boy. In 1845, he published his autobiography, *Narrative of the Life of Frederick Douglass, an American Slave, Written by Himself,* describing his life and inner struggles against bondage. Many readers doubted that an ex-slave could really write so well. During the Civil War he became an adviser to President Lincoln and helped to recruit northern African Americans to serve in the Union army.

After the Civil War, he worked for equal rights for blacks, American Indians, women, and the poor. He understood how all suppressed people suffered. About his life as a slave he said in his book, "I longed to have a future—a future with hope in it."

and the newly organized Confederate states. Tennessee, like Virginia, North Carolina, and Arkansas, did not join the Confederacy until after the fighting began. Master Love then went off to join General Robert E. Lee's Confederate army and took Sampson Love with him to help build forts for the Confederacy. Gossip was the only way the slaves learned what was happening between the Union and Confederate forces. The slave owners in Nat's neighborhood told their slaves that if the Union soldiers caught them, they would hang them. They hoped the stories would keep their slaves from running away.

Still, Nat and the other slave children hoped the Union forces would win. On their Sundays off, the slave boys now played war. Since all the boys wanted to be Yankees and none wanted to be Confederates, they had to find other enemies. Gathering sticks, old rags, rocks, and brooms, the boys set off over the fields and roads in search of an enemy. They soon found a nest of yellow jackets, and they attempted to destroy them with their weapons. Many of the "soldiers," including Nat, received "wounds" from their attack on the yellow jackets, but in the end they were able to capture what they termed "Fort Hell." They called this the "Battle of the Wilderness," and each Sunday after that, the boys marched out in search of new territory and new enemies. In one battle with bees, Nat's nose and eyes swelled so much he could hardly see for several days. Nat was learning to be tough.

## BATTLE OF SHILOH

During the Civil War, in February 1862, Union forces won important battles in northern Tennessee. Union commander Ulysses S. Grant captured Fort Donelson and soon moved his troops into southern Tennessee. After this, the first of the Civil War's huge bloody battles took place. Known as the Battle of Shiloh, the Union troops lost more than 13,000 men, either killed, severely wounded, or captured. The Confederacy lost 11,000 men, and neither side claimed victory. The loss of men in this one battle was greater than those in the Revolutionary War, the War of 1812, and the War with Mexico combined. As noted in Mary Beth Norton's *A People and a Nation*, when this terrible clash ended, Grant said, "I saw an open field over which confederates had made repeated charges..., so

Due to the declining number of white volunteers, the pressing needs of the Union army, and the passing of the Emancipation Proclamation, black men (who previously had been forbidden to serve in the U.S. army, although blacks had fought in the American Revolution and the War of 1812) volunteered for service in large numbers. By the end of the Civil War, about 179,000 black men served as soldiers in the U.S. army and another 19,000 served in the navy.

covered with dead that it would have been possible to walk across the clearing, in any direction, stepping on dead bodies, without a foot touching the ground."

After this horrific battle, Master Love allowed Sampson to return home. Before long, Union soldiers passed through the neighborhood on their way south. The slaves found that the soldiers did not harm them as their masters had warned, but instead they took whatever supplies they could. The plantations in the area were soon left with few provisions and food became scarce.

During the war years, President Abraham Lincoln issued proclamations freeing the slaves in the territories of the Confederate states. Neither Master Love nor any of the other slave owners ever mentioned this in front of their slaves. According to Nat, his family only learned that they had been freed after the war ended. Thousands of other slaves who lived close to war zones escaped to freedom by crossing into Union territory. Many of the African-American men worked in Union camps, and eventually more than 190,000 African Americans, both ex-slaves and freedmen, were allowed to join the Union army and navy. In segregated units, they helped bring the eventual Union victory. Despite black troops' bravery in battle, racism remained strong in the Union army. *A People and a Nation* told of one white soldier who wrote home: "I never came out here for to free the black devils."

And yet, most white men in the Union army, especially officers of the African-American troops, experienced for the first time a close relationship with people of color. Many soldiers changed their feelings after fighting in battles alongside comrades with brown skin. As written by Norton, one white man wrote his wife: "I have a more elevated opinion of their abilities than I ever had before."

In January 1865, when it looked like the Union forces would achieve victory, the U.S. Congress passed the Thirteenth Amendment to the U.S. Constitution outlawing slavery or "involuntary servitude" in the United States. The amendment also said U.S. government officials could enforce this measure by "appropriate legislation [laws]." The Civil War ended formally on April 9, 1865, when Confederate general Robert E. Lee surrendered to Union lieutenant general Ulysses S. Grant at the Appomattox Court House in Virginia. Union troops would remain in the states of the old Confederacy to enforce the U.S. Constitution and help set up new state governments. Although President Lincoln had guided the nation through the war and brought victory to the Union, he was killed by an assassin's bullet just five days later. John Wilkes Booth, a Southern sympathizer and actor, entered Lincoln's box seat at the Ford's Theatre in Washington, D.C., during a performance of *Our American Cousin* and shot Lincoln in the head. The nation mourned Lincoln's sudden death. For Nat's family and the other ex-slaves, Lincoln remained a hero. He was the president who had given precious freedom to the slaves.

Many slaves upon hearing the news of their emancipation set off immediately to find lost family members. A few headed out West, hoping to start a new life. Others sang and rejoiced for days. One old woman stood in the field hoeing when she heard the news. She threw down her hoe and ran to find her mistress. As Norton wrote, when she faced her, she screamed, "I'm free! Yes, I'm free! Ain't got to work for you no more!"

At the end of the war, a new life began for Nat and his family, too. They were free to live on their own. But where would they go? What could they do?

# FREEDOM AT LAST

Nat Love and his family were no longer slaves, but just like other newly freed people, they had no money or resources. For this reason some African Americans decided to stay and work for their former masters in exchange for food and a place to live. Sampson was ambitious, and he wanted to become a farmer. He arranged to rent 20 acres (8 hectares) of land from his former master near their slave cabin, which Master Love allowed them to keep. Nat, Sampson, and Jordan began to clear the land for planting. Nat's sister, Sally, had married another ex-slave and they, too, rented land to farm a few miles away. Like many other freedmen they became tenant farmers, which meant they paid rent on their land after their crops were harvested. Others known as sharecroppers gave a percentage of their crop, sometimes almost half, to the landowner.

## LIFE AS TENANT FARMERS

The Love family was free but also hungry and poor. Nat's mother was reduced to making "ash cakes" to feed her boys and husband. First, she got credit to buy buttermilk and bran, which she mixed with water. Then she baked the dough on a cabbage leaf in the ashes from their fireplace. This was the only food they ate for weeks. The Loves still wore the clothes they had worn as slaves, and Nat had

26

only one shirt. At night, his mother washed it so it would be clean for the next day.

The Loves worked as hard as they had when they were slaves, but now it was for themselves. The land around the cabin was overgrown with weeds and bramble, and was difficult to clear. Once Sampson, Nat, and Jordan had removed all the brush, they began to plow the fields. After the sun went down each day, and it was too dark to work in the fields, Sampson sat in the cabin and twisted brooms from the straw Nat and Jordan had gathered during the day. The boys also helped their father gather reeds and cut cane stalks to weave into seats for chairs. With a load of brooms and cane seats, Sampson set off each Friday afternoon to Nashville, a 12-mile (10-kilometer) walk. He was usually able to sell his wares and with the money Sampson bought food for the family and seeds for his crops.

In the field, Sampson laid out straight rows, and Nat and Jordan followed, dropping in corn kernels; then, Sampson walked behind and covered the corn kernels with soil. Besides corn, they planted tobacco and vegetables. Finally after several weeks, the corn and vegetables began to ripen, Nat was delighted when they had something to eat besides ash cakes.

Tobacco was the cash crop they planted to make money for the family. When the tobacco plants came up, Nat and Jordan helped transplant them into new rows. As the little plants grew, the boys cut off the sucker leaves and got rid of worms. The worst part, Nat thought, was pulling the worms off the leaves. They were ugly, and Nat and Jordan used a stick to knock them off, but when their father saw this, he scolded them. As they knocked off the worms with the stick, Sampson explained, they also took off a few of the valuable leaves. As distasteful as it was, Nat and Jordan walked the field and plucked off the fat worms by hand, one by one. As the tobacco leaves ripened, they had to be cut and then cured and stacked before they could be sold. Growing tobacco was strenuous work, and the first year's crop was small. Despite how hard they had worked that spring and summer, most of the money they made went to Master Love to pay the rent on the land.

Once they were free, Nat Love and his family worked for their former master as tenant farmers. Many former slaves became tenant farmers and sharecroppers because they owned no land and were penniless. Tenant farmers were a step above sharecroppers on the agricultural ladder because they owned their own tools and owed less to the landowner. Above, the son of sharecropper Billy Compton works in a strip house in North Carolina, taking tobacco off a drying stand for grading and stripping.

The hard winter of 1865–1866 followed for the Love family; they still had little food. With nothing to do in the fields, Sampson made both Nat and Jordan work on their writing and reading. In the spring, Sampson went to work for a nearby planter in exchange for the use of his horse and plow. Sampson plowed more land than the year before, but soon afterward he became ill and took to his bed. With no money for a doctor, after a few weeks Sampson died. Nat mourned the loss of his dear father; he had looked up to him and would miss

# Emancipation Proclamations

When the Civil War began in 1861, many people in the North wondered what would happen to the slaves held inside the Confederate States of America. Abolitionists were angry and disappointed that President Abraham Lincoln failed to outlaw slavery everywhere as soon as the Civil War broke out. Instead, Lincoln waited until after the Union army's victory at the Battle of Antietam in September 1862 to declare a two-part proclamation of freedom for the slaves. He used his powers as commander in chief of the armed forces to proclaim freedom for all slaves in Confederate states unless those states returned to the Union by January 1, 1863. On that date, Lincoln gave a second order freeing all slaves in the states fighting against the Union.

Many people in the North criticized Lincoln, saying the Emancipation Proclamation only affected slaves in the Confederate states, where the United States had no control. It was unclear what would happen to slaves held in the Union states. Still, the Emancipation Proclamation became an important document for many reasons. It encouraged slaves in the Confederate states to escape to Union territory where they would be free. Thousands "voted with their feet" and walked to free states and reached Union lines. With each new territory taken by the Union army, more slaves gained freedom.

The Emancipation Proclamation of 1863 also was a legal document stating that the war against the Confederate States of America was a war against slavery. This gave a new moral direction to the Civil War. By the spring, black troops began fighting for the Union with the hope that they could gain citizenship and full rights for freed blacks. The war finally ended April 9, 1865, but it was not until December 18, 1865, that the U.S. Congress passed the Thirteenth Amendment to the Constitution outlawing slavery.

his love and attention. The misery was not over. A short time later, Sally's husband died. Sally and her two young daughters came to live in the Love family cabin. It was a sad time for the whole family.

With help from Sally, Nat and Jordan planted, weeded, and hoed all day trying to keep up with the crops, but the work was too much. Their food crops gave them enough to eat, but when they harvested the tobacco, sold it, and paid their rent, they again ended up with little cash. Then Sally grew sick. She, too, died, leaving behind her two young girls.

## FINDING A JOB

Nat realized there would not be enough food to last the winter and his little nieces needed clothing to stay warm and healthy. He had turned 13 years old that spring, and he decided to find a job wherever he could. He later wrote in his autobiography, "The fact that I was now free, gave me a new born courage to face the world."

Nat walked from farm to farm asking for work. Eventually, he found a job for $1.50 a month, working for Mr. Brooks whose farm was about six miles (9 km) from home. Though the wage was low, Nat felt proud that he would soon be able to buy food to feed his family. After one week on the job, Nat found ways to collect a few potatoes, some cornmeal, and molasses to take home. Neighbors of Mr. Brooks also gave Nat some old clothes, which his mother mended for the little girls. Nat worked hard to do the chores well, and by his third month his wages were raised to $3.00. Though food and clothing remained scarce, Nat used some of his pay to buy a book for each of his little nieces. He read to them and taught them how to read. He believed in the value of learning to read and write, but in his town there were no schools for African-American children.

The future seemed bright to Nat as he started his fourth month at the Brooks farm, but at the end of that month Mr. Brooks gave him only 50 cents, saying he had already drawn his wages. Nat was angry and upset, but he knew that a young black boy had no power against a white farmer. By then, spring was on the way, and there was plenty of plowing and planting to keep both him and Jordan busy all day on the Love's land.

# BREAKING HORSES

Despite the long hours of work, on Sundays Nat and Jordan took the day off. Tennessee had several horse farms, and the South had a tradition of African-American stable boys, trainers, and even jockeys for the racehorses. Nat had always liked horses and would often go to the horse farm owned by the Williams family, not far from his cabin. The Williams brothers were about Nat's age, and they usually let him ride their horses. He loved riding, and one day the oldest Williams boy asked if Nat could help break in, or tame, the young horses for riding. Nat was only too happy to help, and the Williams boys agreed to pay him 10 cents for each colt he broke. The next Sunday when Mr. and Mrs. Williams went off to church, Nat started his new job. Although they were all excited, the Williams boys were unsure if their father would approve of their plan so they had to be careful in case Mr. Williams returned home unexpectedly. They said that Nat could not use a bridle which meant he would have to try riding the young horses without a bridle or a saddle. He would have to stay on by just holding the horse's mane.

The boys drove the first colt into the barn and into a stall. From the side of the stall, Nat tried to get on the horse's back and grab its neck hairs. Nat lifted up his leg and finally straddled the colt, holding tight to the mane. The boys slid back the pole and opened the door, and the colt bolted from the barn. Nat made it into the barnyard hanging on with both hands. The horse jumped and bucked again and again, but Nat used his arms and legs to cling to the colt's sides and back—up into the air and down. Finally the poor colt grew tired and let his rider control him. When Nat jumped down, he was paid 10 cents.

Each Sunday after that, as Mr. and Mrs. Williams left for church, Nat broke another colt. The sons paid Nat, who loved both the challenge and the money. After he had tamed about 12 young horses, the Williams boys asked Nat to try to ride a full-grown horse called the Black Highwayman. This horse was mean and wild. He was tall

Before a horse will allow itself to be harnessed or ridden, sometimes it will reject the rider. Horse trainers must "break" the horse, a process of training the horse to submit to human riders. One technique, used by horse trainers, is simply to throw a saddle onto the horse and ride until its will to resist is finally broken.

and looked much angrier than any of the colts he had tamed. Nat knew the black horse was a real threat, and he could get badly hurt if he was thrown. Still, he decided he would try because he needed the money. He asked for 50 cents to ride the big horse; the boys finally agreed to 25 cents, paid in advance—whatever happened.

The boys had a hard time getting Black Highwayman into the stall in the barn, and Nat had trouble getting on his back. He finally managed to do it and he later described his ride in his book:

> Out of the barn we shot like a black cloud, around the yard we flew, then over the garden fence. Over the fields we went, the horse clearing the highest fences and other obstacles in his way…. All the dogs in the neighborhood were fast joining in the race…. After about 2 miles [3.2 kilometers] we cleared a fence into a pasture where

there was a large number of other horses…, who promptly stampeded as we joined them. Naturally we formed
quite a spectacle that could not fail to attract the attention of the neighbors, who as soon as possible mounted
horses and started in pursuit and vainly tried to catch
my black mount but could get nowhere near him….

Finally, Black Highwayman slowed and stopped, sweating and
exhausted. Nat had managed to hold on through the entire ride, but
when he checked for the quarter (which he had tied in the corner of
his shirt) it was gone. He felt as if he had risked his life for nothing.
The Williams boys refused to pay him another quarter. Later Mr.
Williams heard about the wild ride and found it quite funny. Every-
one in the neighborhood now knew Nat could break a horse.

Besides breaking horses and doing the work around the Love
farm, in the spring Nat helped his family gather wild berries growing in the woods near their cabin. They collected big basketsful and
took them to town to sell, along with early cucumbers. In the fall,
they gathered walnuts, hickory nuts, and chestnuts in the woods.
Nat built a kind of box sleigh with a rope to pull the baskets of nuts
and vegetables to market. Although they remained poor, they were
no longer needy and had enough to eat. Nat was growing stronger
and more muscular.

By the time Nat turned 14 years old, he had probably heard
something of African-American cowboys who rode the range
in western states and territories. He knew his brother Jordan was
strong and healthy and could do the hard labor on the farm by himself. Nat considered leaving home and going west. As he wrote in his
book, "It was hard to think of leaving mother and the children, but
freedom is sweet and I wanted to make more of the opportunity and
my life than I could see possible around home."

## JOHNSON HORSE RAFFLE

Poor as he was there seemed little hope, though, that Nat could find
a way to earn enough money to go to the West. Still he read all he

could and talked to all of his neighbors. One day, Nat heard about a neighbor, Mr. Johnson, who announced he would hold a horse raffle for his fine horse at 50 cents a ticket. Nat immediately bought one ticket. His name was drawn, and he won the horse. Mr. Johnson then told Nat he would buy the horse back for $50. Since Nat could use the money more than a horse, he agreed. According to Nat, Mr. Johnson again raffled the horse and a second time he entered the raffle and won. His luck seemed too good to be true (and perhaps it was). Once more, Mr. Johnson offered to buy back the horse, and Nat agreed. With his new fortune, Nat hurried home with $100.

He pleaded with his mother to let him go out west and try to improve himself. He gave her $50 and with the rest, he said, he could travel to Kansas. She begged him not to leave, so he agreed to stay for a while. Within a month, an uncle came to live on the farm to help out. Now, Nat knew his family could manage without him. He went to town and bought underwear, shoes, and clothes for traveling. He believed he had everything he needed to find a new life. With mixed feelings of joy and sadness, Nat said good-bye to his mother, brother, nieces, and the farm and, as he said in his book, "started out for the first time alone in a world I knew very little about."

# OFF TO THE WEST

Although Love's life was about to change, he had no idea how great that change would be. He was living through what later historians would call the Reconstruction Period. In 1867, the politicians in Congress had passed the Reconstruction Act, which divided the South into five military districts. This act imposed martial law and set down requirements for the Southern states to rejoin the Union. Each state had to ratify, or uphold, the Fourteenth Amendment and write a new state constitution guaranteeing universal male suffrage, meaning voting rights to all men. Love had probably never heard the term *reconstruction*, but as an adolescent, he had endured hard times with his family on their rented land. By leaving his birthplace, he hoped to find something different—away from bigoted attitudes and treatment toward freedmen, away from poverty, away from the life of a sharecropper or tenant farmer. Like his father, he was both ambitious and intelligent, and he had no intention of being held down because he was African American.

## LEAVING HOME

Love set out for the West on February 10, 1869, just four months before his fifteenth birthday. He must have been both excited and fearful of what lay ahead. Gossip and word of mouth as well as drawings and newspaper articles described the frontier of the Wild

The Oregon, California, Mormon, Santa Fe, and Pony Express trails were the most common overland routes to the West. On these trails, travelers like Nat Love followed various rivers, passed towering bluffs, and fought off attacks by Native Americans. Although Love was traveling alone, he saw groups of families riding across the plains in covered wagons like the one shown above.

West. Love was strong and eager to see what the frontier could offer him. He started off on foot, carrying his worldly possessions and heading into an unknown land. At first, the roads and farms looked familiar, for Tennessee was still mostly horse country and tobacco farms. In Missouri, the landscape began to change. By hitching occasional rides from farmers, Love made his journey across Tennessee, Missouri, and finally into Kansas.

The country Love traveled through was filled with wild ducks, pheasant, herds of elks and antelope, and even prairie dogs, as the trees gave way to prairies. The prairie grasses seemed to go on

forever across the flatlands. Occasional cottonwoods grew along
the banks of streams and rivers. Love walked through dust, mud,
gnats, mosquitoes, hailstorms, and strong winds. Spring storms
with clapping thunder and flashing lightning brought heavy rains,
and there was little shelter. The streams and rivers rose above their
banks, and crossing on foot proved cold and difficult. At some rivers, ferries took passengers across for a fee. Love had to decide if he
would part with some of his valuable money or try the crossing on
his own. Along the way, he passed small towns with sod houses and
public springs where clean water could be had. Wagonloads of families hoping for a better life rolled along the trails. In places, grave
markers of earlier travelers lined the rutted roads. During the Civil
War in 1862, the U.S. Congress had passed the Homestead Act, of-
fering cheap or free land to settlers who would go west to farm and
improve the open countryside. Earlier pioneers had named the
landscape: Diamond Springs for its sparkling waters, Plum Buttes
with wild plum bushes growing on tall sand dunes, Walnut Creek
with the tall trees around it, Black Pool whose shale shelf made the
drinking water look black until it hit the sunlight. Each day brought
some new sight. Everything Love saw seemed unfamiliar and fresh
to a boy leaving his family and home for the first time.

In Kansas, Camp Grierson, near the Little Arkansas River, had
been manned by the black regiment of the U.S. 10th Cavalry just two
years before Love arrived. Some of the African-American soldiers
had been killed by Native Americans as the soldiers tried to protect
the river crossing. Others had died of cholera while stationed at the
camp. Just four years before Love arrived, Fort Dodge opened along
the Santa Fe Trail to protect wagon trains, stagecoaches, railroad
construction crews, and the U.S. mail. The fort served as a base for
U.S. troops fighting tribes such as the Cheyenne and Kiowa, trying
to remove them from their traditional homelands. By the time Love
entered Kansas, most Native Americans were being forced onto reservations, usually covering only a small section of their ancestral
homelands.

In April 1869, after walking for several weeks, Love's journey led him to a bustling cattle town. Cattle pens surrounded the

## Buffalo Soldiers

During the Civil War, Negro, or colored troops, as they were then called, fought bravely for the Union. They battled in segregated units, and after the war, in 1866, the U.S. Congress recognized their valor as well as the need to make the western territories safe for the white settlers who streamed across the plains. Congress then authorized the organization of four African-American regiments, the 24th and 25th Infantries and the 9th and 10th Cavalries. Government leaders sent these African-American men to fight in the West where conflicts often arose between white settlers and Native Americans, whose lands were being invaded. It may seem strange that many of those who had recently been enslaved were sent to help defeat the Native Americans, but they, too, quickly adopted prejudicial attitudes against Native American people. These African-American troops helped to make the new territories safe for the whites who settled them.

The 9th and 10th Calvaries made up 20 percent of the U.S. Cavalry in the West. Although some white officers refused to be assigned to these

Pictured are buffalo soldiers of the 25th Infantry in Fort Keough, Montana.

outskirts, and he passed by camps of cowboys. As Love entered the town, he found the street lined with dance halls, saloons, gambling houses, and outfitter stores where a cowboy could buy all he needed.

cavalry units, the African Americans soon achieved a reputation for their brav-ery and skill. Their duty was to patrol from the Rio Grande River on the border with Mexico to the northern border with Canada. Besides protecting settlers and chasing hostile Native Americans, these troops also scouted for cattle thieves, gave escort to wagon trains, cattle herds, surveying parties, and stage coaches, and acted as guards along the Rio Grande and other important river crossings, defending the western plains.

From the beginning they were given the most dangerous and difficult tasks and, often, poor equipment. According to *The Black West* by William Loren Katz, one of their white officers said that his "regiment has received nothing but broken-down horses and repaired equipment." Yet the black men soon won the respect of the Native American people. For their coura-geous fighting and their short, curled hair, the Native Americans gave them the name "buffalo soldiers." It was a title filled with honor as the buffalo was considered sacred by many of the Native Americans. The men of the 9th and 10th Calvaries took pride in the name. The 10th Cavalry soon put the buffalo at the top of their military crest.

The buffalo soldiers continued to serve with honor and distinction, de-spite the rising sentiments against African Americans and growing segrega-tion in the country. As Katz wrote, buffalo soldier sergeant Moses Williams won the Medal of Honor because he "...skillfully conducted a running fight of three or four hours, and by his coolness, bravery and unflinching devotion to duty in standing by his commanding officer in an exposed position under heavy fire from a large party of Indians, saved the lives of at least three of his comrades."

By the end of the frontier days, buffalo soldiers had earned 11 Medals of Honor for their heroism. Yet African-American soldiers continued to fight in segregated units until after World War II. Finally, in 1948, President Harry Truman brought about racial desegregation of the armed forces. The buf-falo soldiers, though, had made their history in the Wild West.

He found African-American, white, and Mexican cowboys swarm-ing the town. They had just brought herds of cattle from Texas and the western territories to this railroad town. It was a market town where big steers brought $40 to $60 a head and were eventually sent out over the recently built railroad to a nation eager for beef. When Love arrived, the town seemed so wild and reckless with gamblers, fistfights, knife fights, the sound of occasional gunshots, and rough and drunken men roaming the streets that he felt uneasy. He was afraid to ask anyone about how he might find a job. He decided to wait and go the next morning to one of the cowboy camps on the outskirts of town.

# RED RIVER DICK

In the morning, he found a camp of about 15 cowboys sitting around eating breakfast; some of the men were African American. Someone called to him to come over and join them. Love was delighted. He soon found out they were the Duval outfit from the Panhandle of Texas, with their home ranch along the Palo Duro River. They had just driven a herd of cattle all the way from Texas. It was sold, and they would be returning to the ranch the next day. Love longed to work with this outfit. After breakfast, he found the boss and asked if he might have a job. According to Love, as written in his book, the boss asked Love, could he ride a wild horse?

"Yes, sir," Love answered.

So the boss called to Jim Bronko, an African-American cowboy. "Go out and get old Good Eye, saddle him and put Love on his back."

Before Love mounted the horse, Bronko gave him a few pointers. Still when Love got on, he had a tough ride. It seemed the horse pitched and bucked more than any he had ridden before, but he managed to wear Good Eye down and stay in the saddle. The boss was impressed and offered him a job for $30 per month. Love was overjoyed. In his book, Love said he remembered later, that when the boss "asked what my name was and I answered Nat Love, he said to the boys we will call him Red River Dick."

Having a nickname was a cowpuncher's tradition, and Love proudly went by that name for a long time. After hiring him, the boss took Love into town to one of the outfitter stores. He gave him an advance on his pay to buy his cowboy gear: a saddle, bridle, spurs, chaps, boots with tall heels to stay in the stirrups, a couple of blankets, bandanas, and a .45 Colt revolver. Love had never shot a gun before, but he strapped his new six-shooter to his waist like all the other cowboys. Now he was outfitted like a real cowpuncher and one of the crew.

The next day as they saddled up and started back for Texas, Love promised himself he would do anything he had to so he could stay with this outfit. The men he rode with were all experienced and friendly. Only a few miles from town along the trail, they ran into a band of Victoria Indians. These were the first Native Americans Love had ever seen, and he watched them race toward him. As he later recalled, "When I saw them coming after us and heard their blood curdling yells, I lost all courage and thought my time had come to die. Some of the boys told me to use my gun and shoot for all I was worth."

It was a short battle, as the Victoria stampeded all but six of the crew's extra horses. One of the cowhands riding near Love was shot off his horse. As the band raced away with their horses, the men saw they had lost one of their own. Love watched as they wrapped him in his blanket and dug a grave on the open plains, marking it with a pile of stones. So many thoughts rushed through Love's head, so many extraordinary experiences for a 15-year-old boy who had left the plantation only weeks before. For Love it was a life-changing experience. He later said, "After this engagement with the Indians I seemed to lose all sense as to what fear was."

# A COWPUNCHER

Following the trail toward the Duval ranch took several weeks. This gave Love time to start learning to be a cowpuncher. Already he was a good horseman, but now he had to pick up the other skills as well. Each fall, the crew he rode with drove herds of cattle to the Kansas towns of Abilene, Wichita, Ellsworth, or Dodge City. When riding the trail with their herds, Love learned, the cowboys spent 14 to 18 hours each day in the saddle, and at night they made a campfire, ate their dinner, unrolled their blankets, and slept on the ground. It was easy to see why many of the old cowboys were bowlegged from their many hours on horseback. As Love discovered, the days were long and the work sweaty and hard.

During the day, each cowpuncher rode in a different position. The drover, or trail boss, was in charge and usually rode in front of the herd. With each cowboy in charge of about 250 head of cattle, the line of bellowing steers often spread as wide as two miles (3.2 km) as it moved through the rugged country up the trail. Alongside the herd rode the flank riders, whose job it was to keep the cattle from wandering away from the group. Behind all the cattle trotted the drag rider who kept the herd moving forward and was constantly "eating dust." The wrangler was in charge of the extra horses, for each man needed three to six horses for the long drives, which often covered more than 1,200 miles (1,931 km). This herd of horses was called the remuda, and the wrangler brought them into the camp early each morning so the cowboys could choose a fresh horse. In the beginning of his cowboy years, horses were all Love knew, so he probably started as a wrangler.

One of the most important crew members was the cook, who drove the chuck wagon ahead to the night's camping place. Depending on the ruggedness of the trail and the weather, the herd covered about 15 to 20 miles (24 to 32 km) each day. The cook kept the chuck wagon loaded with the supplies of food and medicines needed along the way. He baked bread and biscuits in a cast iron pot hanging over the campfire and cooked beans, bacon, salt pork, and an occasional pie made with dried or canned fruit. He served strong hot coffee with each meal. The wrangler and cowboys brought him wood and buffalo chips to build his fires.

Each night, the cattle were stopped to graze while the cowboys slept. A couple of the men had to patrol the herd on the night watch while the others slept. After a quick breakfast in the morning, the crew got the cattle moving up the trail again.

Although Love was a good rider, he was considered a greenhorn, one who was new to the job. Love watched and listened to the crew as they taught him the skills he needed. With his lariat

With the settlement of Texas in the 1840s and the expansion of the north and west through to the 1880s, ranching was crucial to the western economy. This photograph from 1898 shows a number of cowboys on horseback and a herd of cattle in a shallow valley in Colorado.

tied to his saddle horn he practiced roping, finally getting the lasso to land where he wanted it. With a slipknot he expanded the loop to make it bigger and bigger, and then one day, he whirled it over the head of a horse. Once he could do that, Love practiced and practiced and eventually he could rope a running steer from his galloping horse.

At the end of May, they reached the home ranch. Love found what was a typical cattle ranch, stretching for miles over the open range. Though the surrounding countryside was dry and covered with brush and grass, the ranch house stood a short distance from the Palo Duro River. In addition to the wide grasslands where the livestock grazed, water was essential for thirsty cattle. As for the cowboys, they ate their meals in a kitchen, or mess hall, in this house and slept in the bunkhouse. Even when they remained at the home ranch, the cowpunchers worked hard. The horses had to be trained to help on the cattle drives. Some horses learned to follow a steer that needed to be cut, or separated, from the herd. Other horses could be taught to lead the herd across rivers. The corrals for training the horses had to be repaired, as did the chuck wagon. Horses needed new shoes, quirts (whips) had to be woven, the barn kept clean, and grazing herds of younger cattle checked on. Love had to keep his new cowboy gear in good condition. His saddle was his most expensive piece of equipment, and to keep the leather from drying out, he rubbed it with a special soap. Along with others, Love often rode out for days, moving large herds of cattle from one grazing place to another. At times, the boys had to search for stray cattle, which wandered into box canyons, rock crevices, and even snowbanks in winter. Sometimes they went out and rounded up broncos to add to their supply of horses. In the evening, in the bunkhouse or around the campfire, Love listened to stories of past cattle drives and tall tales of cowboy escapades. After supper, the boys might play dominoes, mumblety-peg (a knife-tossing game), or card games. Occasionally a cowboy played the banjo, the fiddle, or even the mouth organ [harmonica]. Still, after a long day, sleep came easily.

Although Love had never shot a gun before joining the Duval outfit, with the death of a fellow cowboy he had already seen the importance of learning to shoot. When a mountain lion or other animal would attack the herd, some of the boys had to go out and hunt it down. Love acquired a Winchester rifle for shooting wolves, bears, coyotes, or wild game to eat. Like his new companions, Love took every opportunity to practice with his .45 Colt revolver. Soon he felt proud that he could hit the barn door if "it was not too far away." Over time, with more practice he became an accurate shot with both his rifle and his .45 Colt revolver.

Despite missing his devoted mother, Love's new life pleased him greatly. He said in his book, "The life was hard and in some ways exacting…, and contained elements of danger which my nature craved…. I gloried in the danger, and the wild and free life of the plains, the new country I was continually traversing and the many new scenes and incidents continually arising in the life of a rough rider."

# THE WILD AND RUGGED WEST

In the fall of 1872, Love returned to his home ranch from a long drive north and decided to accept an offer of work from Pete Gallinger, who ran a cattle ranch along the Gila River in Arizona Territory. The job offered him more pay, and besides, he had turned 18 years old in the spring and was restless for new experiences. So, after three years, Love said a sad farewell to the men of the Duval outfit who had helped him gain his skills as a cowboy and rode off to the desert range. With his new outfit, he traveled the West from the Missouri state line to the Pacific Ocean and from Mexico to the Dakotas. He herded cattle over dry sands, past alkaline water holes, through mountain ranges, past army posts, by copper and silver mines, and along such well-known trails as the Chisholm, Western, Goodnight-Loving, and the old Hays and Ellsworth trails, some heading across Indian Territory (now Oklahoma) and others through the lands of the Apache, Navajo, Sioux, and Comanche. Love faced more than one skirmish with Native Americans. The U.S. government leaders were relentless in their attempt to get all the tribes onto reservations. The tribes fought bravely, but they were outnumbered by the advancing settlers, miners, and cattlemen who had the U.S. soldiers to protect them. According to *The*

*Negro Cowboys* by Philip Durham and Everett L. Jones, before the Battle of the Little Big Horn in 1876 Sitting Bull told his men, "Be brave my children. Your wives and little ones are like birds without a nest."

## THE ROUNDUP

Without fences to hold them in, cattle grazed freely on the wide open lands of the Southwest. The scrublands provided winter and summer pastures to fatten the cows and Texas longhorn steers before they were rounded up and herded to market towns and slaughterhouses. As Americans' demand for beef grew, cattle barons grew wealthy with their trade. Love's outfit often delivered horses and cattle to other ranchers as well as to market, so he became especially familiar with Texas, Arizona, New Mexico, the Indian Territory, and Mexico.

Roundups took place in the beginning of April and in the fall. Often they lasted for weeks and covered hundreds of miles as the cowboys tried to gather onto their home range the cattle, which had wandered off in all directions. The vastness of the land meant livestock from different ranches often mingled together and could only be identified by their brands. Each ranch burned its own brand onto its cattle so the cowboys could tell which animals belonged to which rancher. In Arizona, Love's outfit used the half circle box brand. Cattle never liked to be driven from their grazing grounds, but a few cowboys usually started the main herds toward their home territory. Other men stayed to find the rest of their livestock. It was hot, strenuous work to cut a steer from a group of others. Love trained his horses for just this purpose, and the horses were quick to turn and able to follow a particular longhorn steer.

Besides helping to round up the longhorns, and sometimes herds of horses, cowboys searched for mavericks—unbranded animals—and newborn calves to mark. Then, too, there were always those strays which had wandered far away and had to be found, for the loss of even a few steers meant lost money to the rancher. Love once said hunting up strays was a difficult task, for they might roam

Rounding up cattle was strenuous, tiring work. Large numbers of cattle, owned by different ranchers, roamed the open range and mingled together. In order to determine ownership, ranchers marked their cattle with a distinctive brand while the cattle were still young calves. This calf has been marked by an eartag and a brand to identify its owner.

for miles and miles before he located and rounded them up to return to the main herd.

## BRAND READER

Love had gained the skills of a cowboy, and with his natural curiosity he continued to learn new things. During his time as a cowpuncher, he had met Mexican *vaqueros* (cowboys) and other ranch hands who spoke Spanish, and he learned to speak it well. It helped him in his dealings with other cowboys or when his outfit picked up herds from Mexico. Many cowboys—African American, Anglo, or Mexican American—never learned to read or write. Love was accomplished at both, and he could also easily identify the various brands of the Western range. All the large cattle ranches had brand

## Texas Longhorns

Long before cattle grazed on the open ranges of Texas, they roamed the wide valleys and early rancheros (ranches) of Mexico. The explorers and conquistadors from Spain brought cattle with them in the 1500s. Over time, many strays found their way to Texas. When settlers from the United States entered the region, they brought with them European breeds, which mixed with the wild cattle from Mexico and became the Texas longhorn breed. They were hardy and could survive in rough country with sagebrush and cactus, go for days without water, and tolerate blizzards, dust storms, and even drought. The animals had long legs and sturdy feet, and thus could endure the long cattle drives with little weight loss. Their wide horns had sharp points, and the bulls would easily attack if angered.

Early Texas ranchers in the 1830s began to think of herding them to market, and during the Civil War a few were used to feed the Confederate troops. After the Civil War ended in 1865, Texas ranchers like Charles Goodnight and his partner, Oliver Loving, saw the profit that could be made by driving longhorns to the railroad towns like Wichita, Abilene, and Ellsworth, Kansas, and selling them as beef cattle. According to Wayne Gard in *The Chisholm Trail*, Goodnight said of the breed, "As trail cattle, their equal never has been known. Their hoofs are superior to those of any other cattle. In stampedes, they hold together better, are easier to circle during a run and rarely split off when you commence to turn the front. No animal of the cow kind will shift and take care of itself under all conditions as will the Longhorns."

Texas became the center of the cattle industry. Later, ranchers found that crossing Texas longhorns with heavier Angus and Herefords produced fatter animals, which could cope with northern winters and were able to withstand the ticks that plagued longhorns. With new breeds, cattle raising spread across the Great Plains.

readers who attended the big roundups. Love had just worked with his new outfit a short time when he was made its chief brand reader. Not only was Love called to identify his half circle box brand, but he decided if a brand had been altered or counterfeited. Cattle rustlers were always looking to pick up cattle. Love also supervised the branding of the calves, which had been born on the range.

Love had a few boys drive the calves to a location where campfires blazed and branding irons were heated red hot in the fire. Each calf, usually mewling for its mother, was wrestled to the ground and a ranch hand or two held it down. Another cowboy wearing heavy gloves grabbed the sizzling branding iron with the half circle box brand and planted it on the hind flank of the calf, holding it as it scorched into the hide, the smell of burning flesh filling the air. When the calf was unpinned, it jumped up, usually still calling for its mother, and ran off to find her. With this permanent scar, as the calf grew, it could be easily identified as belonging to the Gallinger Company.

Once the branding was completed and most of the herd rounded up, the crew started toward their home range. With his new job, instead of heading home, Love got a fresh horse and galloped on his way again in search of all the cattle that were still missing. Sometimes Apache, Comanche, or outlaws stole them off the range. If this happened, then Love and other brand readers trailed them, riding far and wide, until they caught up with the thieves. As they tried to retake their livestock, a gun battle usually followed. As Love recalled in *The Life and Adventures of Nat Love*, "It then became a case of 'to the victor belongs the spoils,' as there was no law respected in this wild country, except the law of might and the persuasive qualities of the .45 Colt pistol." Love was wounded more than once, but he seemed to heal quickly.

When the general roundup was over and all the cattle accounted for, the ranch hands often took part in cowboy sports or contests. One was to select what Love and others called the 7-YL steer—the wildest and biggest longhorn they could find among the herd. The boys took turns trying to rope and ride this 7-YL steer, which was dangerous and difficult. Many times, Love watched as a horse and his rider were gored by the steer. Still he, too, tried this perilous feat, for if he was successful, Love could claim the valuable animal as his own. "But," he admitted, "it is done more for sports' sake than anything else, and the love of showing off, a weakness of all cowboys more or less."

# CATTLE DRIVES

When the fun was over, it was time to move the herd to market. Love and his companions started on the cattle drive, which lasted two to four months, depending on where they were headed and the size and nature of the herd itself. Herds range from 1,000 to as many as 4,000 head. Some drives include a variety of animals. They might be steers, cows, and calves—a mixed herd which was hard to drive because the longhorns walked faster than cows and the cows might still be calving (birthing), so they could not keep up. More often the herds consisted of just three- or four-year-old steers or even just horses. Cowboys moved their herds across dry sands and when they reached a water hole they made sure the animals drank their fill, getting ready for a long, arid stretch ahead. As they crossed a desolate desert land, the boys might keep the livestock moving even at night, for thirsty cattle seldom settled down. Cowpunchers often sang to the herd to help calm the animals. Along the way, storms and rains frequently brought rivers rushing above their banks, making it difficult to get the herd safely across.

On one long cattle drive from the Mexican border to the Powder River in Wyoming, Love and his crew passed through southern Texas and into Indian Territory with a herd of 500 four-year-old steers. Just before they entered the reservation, a group of Native Americans stopped them and demanded a toll of one steer for crossing their lands. Love's trail boss believed the trail was public land, so he had no intention of paying a toll to pass. The crew and the herd stopped to make camp. Love and the others knew they might be attacked so they posted several guards. The attack came but with only a small group of Native American fighters, who quickly retreated. Love and his companions knew there would be more to come. Each man went to sleep with his boots on and his gun in hand. Love later explained in his autobiography:

> The Indians had secured reinforcements and after dividing in two bands, one band hid in the tall grass in order to pick us off and shoot us as we attempted to hold our

cattle, while the other band proceeded to stampede the herd, but fortunately there were enough of us to prevent the herd from stringing out on us as we gave our first attention to the cattle. Back and forward, through the tall grass, the large herd charged, the Indians being kept too busy keeping out of their way to have much time to bother us.

At daylight the Native Americans disappeared, but the herd appeared crazy, still running around. Finally, they slowed and the cowboys discovered several Native American men had hid in the tall grass near the campground. When the cattle stampeded, they trampled the men who could not escape big steers. It was a terrible sight to see bodies mangled in the field. The trail boss felt it best to drive on quickly, which they did. Passing through Indian Territory could often be an ordeal for the cowboys, but this was an incident Love would never forget.

## BUFFALO ON THE RANGE

During the spring roundups, when Love and the others might be away tracking down strays, they often ran into herds of buffalo. Love and his companions would take out their Winchester rifles and try to shoot one or two. Love once said that a buffalo steak "broiled over coals is a dish fit for the Gods."

In the early 1870s, it was still easy to find herds of buffalo grazing on the grasses in the valleys. If work was slow, the cowboys went looking for sport as well as meat. Instead of shooting buffalo with their rifles, they tried to rope a buffalo and then shoot it with a gun and clean it with a knife. On one such hunt, Love spotted a huge bull and decided to try to bring him down. He twirled his rope over the beast's horns, and then wound the other end of his rope to his saddle horn. His horse stopped and prepared to halt the beast, but the animal was too strong for the horse. The big buffalo kept running and broke the saddle loose from Love's horse, throwing Love to the ground, but his saddle trailed behind the buffalo. Love then

American bison, or buffalo, once roamed the grasslands of the West in massive herds numbering in the millions (some estimate 60 to 100 million). In the mid-nineteenth century bison hunters reduced the numbers to a few hundred. Today, the bison population has increased to an estimated 350,000.

jumped on his horse bareback and followed the buffalo, finally getting alongside and drawing his Colt .45. With several shots into its side, the beast finally dropped dead. Love then reclaimed his saddle, and that night, the men enjoyed a meal of buffalo steaks.

## DEADWOOD DICK

Since his time as a cowboy with the Duval outfit, Love had been known as Red River Dick. He kept that name until the summer of 1876, when he was 22 years old and he and his companions delivered a herd of 3,000 steers to Deadwood, South Dakota. That hot Fourth of July the boys had celebrated with a morning roping contest, which Love had won. He received a prize and the name Deadwood Dick.

By afternoon, the cowboys, miners, and gamblers who had gathered in the town were restless for more entertainment. Some of the cowboys began to grumble that they needed a shooting contest. According to Love, some of the best marksmen, with both rifles and revolvers, gathered to test their skill. Among them were Stormy Jim, who claimed he was the champion; Powder Horn Bill, who bragged that he never missed a shot; White Head, a Native American scout who rarely missed his target; and Love, now known as Deadwood Dick. Out on the open range, the fields were measured in distances of 100 and 250 yards (91 and 228.6 meters) for the rifle. For the Colt .45 the distance was 150 yards (136 meters). Under the rules, each man took 14 shots at both targets with his rifle. With his Colt .45, each man took 12 shots.

As Love remembered it, "I placed every one of my 14 shots with the rifle in the bulls eyes with ease, all shots being made from the hip; but with the .45 Colts I missed it twice, only placing 10 shots in the small circle, Stormy Jim being my nearest competitor, only placing 8 bullets in the bulls eye clear, and the rest being quite close, while with the .45 he placed 5 bullets in the charmed circle."

Again Love was declared the champion, this time of the rifle and revolver. He took pride in his success in the rough town of Deadwood. He also liked his new name.

## LOST ON THE RANGE

After returning from a long cattle drive in 1877, Love was working in the Texas Panhandle with more than 30,000 head of cattle grazing over the wide range. Several huge ranches had their cattle feeding in the Panhandle. During the hot, dry months of July and August, Love and the boys kept busy, and when the fall roundup came, they branded the calves and cut their own cattle out from the herds of other ranches. Once most of the herd was gathered, they drove it toward the winter grazing lands close to the home ranch. After counting the herd they found several steers were missing. The next morning, Love and a few of the others scattered in all directions to hunt down the strays.

Nat Love (*above*) used his skills as a marksman and a cowboy to win a rodeo contest in the rough town of Deadwood, South Dakota. His bronco riding skills earned him the nickname Deadwood Dick.

Love rode off alone looking into small canyons and gorges, up hills and down, searching for hidden steers. After riding hard most of the day, without locating any of the missing cattle, Love found himself in unfamiliar country. He spotted a storm coming, as the sky turned dark. Quickly, clouds descended around him, bringing with them hard rain and sleet. He turned toward the agreed-upon camp-ground, but he could not see more than 50 feet ahead. Riding through the storm, he grew cold and tired but kept going. After a few hours, he came upon a small log cabin by a river. Out of the cabin stepped an old man with long hair and a rifle on his arm. Love stopped his horse and reached up to tip his hat, showing he was a friendly cowpuncher. He then explained he was lost and the old man told him to picket his horse with a rope and stake and come into the cabin.

Once inside the cabin, Love noticed that part of the cabin was built underground, like a sort of dugout. The upper part had circular holes through which the old man could put his gun and shoot. He explained that the holes allowed him to fight off Native Americans who tried to attack. Love saw immediately that it was the home of a trapper, for the walls were covered with the skins of coyotes, bob-cats, buffalo, even rattlesnake skins and rattles. The old man said his name was Cater, and he offered Love dinner and a bed.

Love was grateful and after a warm meal, he lay down on a bed of buffalo robes. By morning, the storm had passed and Cater gave him breakfast. Love said farewell, anxious to meet up with his crew, for he knew the boys would be out looking for him when he had failed to return the night before. Cater packed him some food and headed him off in the direction of the flats where the boys had agreed to meet. The distance, Cater said, was at least a long day's ride. Love rode all day and into the night as rain fell, but he never reached the familiar flatland. He decided to stop and camp, giving his tired horse a chance to rest.

He picketed his horse where it could graze in the grassy patch. Then he took his saddle and placed it nearby, pointing it in the direction he planned to go when he awoke. The clouds had covered the stars and he wanted to continue as best he could in the direction of the flats. He lay down and slept, but he was suddenly awakened by a sharp scream. He jumped up and grabbed his rifle, as his horse reared in fright. The stake that held his horse uprooted, and in an instant his horse galloped away into the night. Love thought only for a second of trying to catch him, but then realized it would be almost impossible. After thinking over what he could do, he decided to shoulder his saddle, for it was far too expensive to leave behind, and he started walking over the prairie in the dark.

Even as the sky grew light, it was a slow, hard trudge over the rugged country. By the next evening, Love had run out of food. Even worse, he still didn't recognize where he was and wondered if he was traveling in the right direction. He plodded over a small rise in the prairie and, there before him, grazed a herd of buffalo. As Love later wrote in his autobiography: "These were the first I had seen since I became lost and the sight of them put renewed life and hope in me as I was then nearly famished."

Love spotted a calf within rifle distance. He laid down his saddle, took up his rifle, and pulled the trigger. The calf fell, but the rest of the herd galloped away. He then went down to the calf and began to carve off some meat with his knife. When he had eaten his fill of raw meat, he cut off two hunks more and tied them to his saddle. He again started off, hoping to reach the flats.

Later, he thought he spotted a line of smoke heading across the prairie toward him. Within minutes heavy snow overtook him, and since he could find no protection from the storm, weary and alone, he lay down on his saddle.

After Love failed to return, his friends had gone out to look for him. When the blizzard hit, they had made a camp and waited it out. When the sky cleared, they noticed a strange white lump far out in the snow. They went over to it across the prairie and discovered Love, his fingers frozen around his saddle horn. They carried him to the chuck wagon and wrapped his frozen body in snow to thaw out slowly as they started toward home.

When Love awoke, he was in the chuck wagon, suffering from the burning pain of frostbite. In the days that followed, he lost each of his fingernails and toenails and the skin on his nose. After a couple of weeks resting in the bunkhouse, he recovered well enough to return to work. He hoped never to be lost and alone on the range again.

# LIFE ON THE RANGE

By the time Love reached his twenty-third birthday, he had gained a reputation as a fine roper and rider and knew the cattle country well. With the talent he showed for his work, he received top wages, and his job took him all over cattle country in the United States and Mexico. Although driving cattle to market or riding the range checking on the herd could be monotonous, he generally liked the work. As he said in his autobiography, "[M]ounted on my favorite horse, my long horsehide lariat near my hand, and my trusty guns in my belt and the broad plains stretching away for miles …, I felt I could defy the world. What man with the fire of life and youth and health … would not enjoy such a life?"

## THE COWBOY LIFE

Love had the talent needed to be a good cowboy and this included his courage to face a stampede of crazed cattle or to travel long miles alone across Indian Territory. His sharp mind made quick decisions and he saved a fellow cowboy from drowning as they crossed a swollen river. Like most black cowboys, Love received the same pay as white cowboys, and he found much less discrimination than he would have elsewhere in the country. Still, discrimination and segregation did exist. For one example, Love could never be a trail boss. At the time, it was believed that if an African American held

A typical cowboy crew consisted of a trail chief, several cowboys, a wrangler to take care of the horses, and a cook. An average crew would have at least two or three black cowboys, like the ones shown above. Although black cowboys were rarely allowed to become trail chiefs, they faced less discrimination along the trail than in other jobs. The demands of the trail required that white and black cowboys rely on each other for safety and supplies.

the job of ranch foreman or trail boss, at some point he might have to deal with a white cowboy who would refuse his authority. Kenneth W. Porter wrote in *The Negro on the American Frontier* about Jim Perry, who worked for years with great success on the XIT ranch in Texas. Perry once said, "If it weren't for my black face I'd have been boss of one of these divisions long ago."

Aside from discrimination for top positions, Love and other African Americans experienced segregation in many other ways in certain cattle towns. When Love entered a gambling saloon, he was treated like anyone else, but he was not allowed to enter dance halls

## African-American Women
## on the Frontier

Like many other adventurous women, African-American women came to the Western frontier seeking better opportunities to make a living. Women were scarce in the early days of the Wild West; the frontier was a society of single men, and the skills of women were needed. A few African-American women lived on the frontier in Western settlements and cattle towns; some were part of African-American pioneer families. By the 1850s, most women who were employed outside their own homes worked as servants for little wages. Like the men, many of these women had been slaves before the Civil War, and after the war ended in 1865, many ex-slaves came west looking for a better life. African-American women generally worked as laundresses, dress-makers, housekeepers, or midwives. Some of these women found success running their own businesses, such as restaurants, hotels, hairdressing par-lors, dress shops, laundries, and boardinghouses. Mary Fields, an ex-slave who journeyed to Montana, became a stagecoach driver and delivered the

Pictured is an African-American pioneer family on the American frontier in 1889.

U.S. mail in Cascade. Other women founded churches, charitable societies, orphanages, schools, and literary clubs. Historian Nell Irvin Painter wrote in *Exodusters*: "Black women were more likely than their white counterparts to be active on the grass roots level in the late nineteenth century. Not only was there a long tradition of black women working alongside men, but in addition, the generations maturing after the Civil War acquired their Western education in coeducational institutions."

African-American women differed from white women in the West in that they tended to be better educated and African-American women settled in urban communities more often than rural ones. They were a majority of the African-American population in cities like Denver, Colorado, and Los Angeles, California. While their Anglo counterparts were generally younger, African-American pioneer women were usually between the ages of 20 and 40. Single African-American men, like Anglo men, were eager to find marriage partners, and often waited for stagecoaches or railroad trains to come into their city, hoping for the arrival of African-American women. The women already living in the West wrote to people in their former hometowns trying to locate possible brides for the single men in their communities. As a result, mail-order brides came to Arizona mining camps where they found men with steady jobs and the opportunity to leave poverty and long hours in the fields behind. They came hoping to find love and a good marriage, and some found what they were looking for. Other women found more hard work, laboring in the home and often raising children from a previous marriage. Yet, on the frontier, black women were twice as likely to be married as Chinese or Native American women.

Life on the frontier was often lonely and tedious, but many African-American women grew to love the pioneer life. Eunice Russell Norris helped her family build its log cabin and became a "Colorado cowgirl." Marguerite Gomez, just 16 when she married a man twice her age, soon learned the skills of a cowgirl, riding alongside the herd and breaking wild horses. In addition, she raised seven children from her husband's first marriage. African-American pioneer women, like those of other races, conquered the unique challenges of the frontier and helped to tame the West.

where white women appeared, or restaurants, or to stay in white-owned hotels. Many of the cowboys, white as well as African American, preferred saving money by sleeping in their own camps on the outskirts of town and buying groceries and eating at the hitching rails or in the saloons. Yet, in his day-to-day riding and roping, Love was treated like all the other cowboys, and he gained affection and respect from his companions on the range.

## CROSSING THE WAKEENY RIVER

In April 1878, Love and his outfit left the home ranch with a small herd of horses heading for a ranch near Junction City, Kansas. After many weeks on the trails, as they finally neared their destination, they stopped for the night. The herd grazed on the open prairie, and Love and the boys slept soundly on their bedrolls while the first night watchmen rode around checking the horses. A violent storm blew up in the dark night, and thunder echoed as lightning lit up the sky. Love awoke to hear the frightened horses in a stampede. He rushed to his horse picketed nearby, and soon all the boys were in the saddle chasing after the horses. The thunder kept up a horrible racket, and heavy rains fell all night and into the morning. The crew did everything they could to keep the herd together and to slow them down. The trick was to get the lead horse to turn back into the herd. As the lead horse galloped into the others, they would mix and slow all the horses down as the herd circled into itself. It took all night to get the herd under control. Then someone noticed that Frank Smith had lost his horse, which had stepped into a prairie-dog hole and fallen. Smith had slipped off, but the horse got up and galloped away with his saddle and bridle. Aside from being embarrassed, Smith was unhurt, but no one could find his horse even in the daylight. Smith had lost his valuable saddle, but he picked another horse from the remuda.

After the boys got their breakfast from the chuck wagon, they continued until they reached the Wakeeny River, near Junction City. The water in the river was high, but the crew got the horses to

Nat Love enjoyed going to the local saloon to relax after the hardships of the cattle drive. Although black cowboys were welcome in the saloon and gambling halls, informal segregation was common, with white cowboys sitting on one end and black cowboys on the other.

start swimming. Then more trouble began. As Love later explained in *The Life and Adventures of Nat Love*:

> I had entered the river and my horse was swimming easily, when on glancing around I saw one of the boys, Loyd Hoedin, go under water. Both man and horse completely disappeared. They soon came up only to disappear again. I saw at once something was wrong so when they came up the second time I threw my rope. It fell near Hoedin, who had the presence of mind to grasp it, and hold on while I snaked both man and horse out to safety.

Love was glad when the harrowing trip ended, and they had safely delivered the herd to the ranch. Tired and muddy from the hard weeks on the trail, the crew received their pay. Then Love and the boys headed to Junction City where they bathed, shaved, put on clean clothes, and celebrated for a couple of days before starting toward home again. Unlike many of his crew, Love always set aside some of his wages to spend in the town and when it was gone, he left the saloons and gambling halls and waited at camp. Though he lived the life of a cowboy, Love remained practical in his decisions about saving for his future.

## LOVE FALLS IN LOVE

Into Love's hardworking life on the range, there now came something new—true love. One area where the color line was important was in relationships between men and women. At a dance at the ranch or any time white women and black men were present, interracial friendships were discouraged. Although some black as well as white cowboys did marry Native American, African-American, or Mexican women, many states, including Texas, had antimiscegenation laws, making it illegal for blacks and whites to marry.

A few African-American women lived on the frontier in western settlements and cattle towns where they were part of black pioneer families, or they worked as cooks, laundresses, housekeepers, nurses, or at brothels—all jobs white women also held on the frontier. Love had had the opportunity to meet some of these women, but he was too busy with roundups, branding cattle, reading brands, and driving herds up the trail to take much notice. That changed, though, on a slow trip back from collecting cattle down in Mexico.

As Love and his outfit passed by an old adobe house on the outskirts of the town, he spotted a pretty young woman working in the yard. He pretended to be thirsty and rode over to ask her for a drink of water. She gave him some water and they talked a bit before Love hurried to rejoin his crew, but he was smitten. The trail followed alongside a railroad track, and Love rode beside the cattle thinking of the beautiful Mexican girl. A small engine approached in the distance, and Love told his companions, "I have roped nearly every-thing that could be roped, so now I am going to rope the engine."

The boys tried to convince him not to try, but Love felt so elated, he was determined to do it. He spurred his horse, lariat in hand, and looped it over the smoke stack. His trained horse dug in on his haunches, but the engine pulled both Love and his horse into the ditch. Luckily the rope broke, and they suffered no more harm than being soundly thrown into the dirt. Love's companions had a good laugh; they were just glad he was unhurt. Love was glad his sweet-heart was not there to see it.

After that, each time he went to Mexico to collect cattle, he rode out to the girl's house. For the first time, Love thought about getting married and changing his life. On his next trip to Mexico, though, he overheard his sweetheart promise her mother she would never go off with a "wild cowboy." Love was heartsick, his hopes faded, and he said farewell to his sweetheart. The next few months were filled with hard work as usual and Love was happy for his work, thinking he was getting over his disappointment. Almost seven months later, his outfit again went to Mexico.

Soon after the boys arrived, Love's sweetheart rode out to the camp looking for him. When he heard she was there, he forgot all his sorrow and ran to her. They made plans for a wedding the next year. Love had decided he would move to Mexico, and they could live together near her mother. The following spring, though, his sweetheart became sick and died. Again Love was heartbroken. As he explained, "Her death broke me all up and after I buried her I became very wild and reckless, not caring what happened to me.... I vainly tried to forget her and my sorrow in the wild life of the plains and [took on] every danger I could find courting death in fights with Indians and Mexicans and dare devil riding on the range."

# RIDING THE RAILS AS A PULLMAN PORTER

By the time Love reached his thirties, the world was changing around him. No longer was the West the wild frontier it had once been. Railroads now crisscrossed the prairies, deserts, and mountains, cutting through old cattle trails. Farmers fenced in their crops and water holes and kept cattle out. In the past, battles, or grazing wars, had broken out between farmers and ranchers, each wanting the land and water for their own uses. Open-range ranching faded as big business ranchers replaced the cattle barons who had started the cattle trade.

Towns that had once been small had grown into huge cities like Denver, San Francisco, Kansas City, Chicago, and St. Louis. Native Americans had been driven from their homes and forced to live on reservations. The superintendent of the 1890 Census declared that the American frontier had closed. If it had not closed, at least it became a place where schools, towns, churches, businesses, and even literary societies flourished. People moving west no longer came in covered wagons, but most often they traveled

By 1890, the American frontier had closed and towns had grown into huge cities like San Francisco and St. Louis *(seen above in 1890)*. In the West, cattle were now enclosed in barbed wire and no longer roamed the plain. As a result, fewer cowboys were needed for roundups and cattle drives. In addition, windmills were used to drive pumps that could pull water from underground, so there was no need to put cattle ranches near a river or stream.

on the railroads. Famous outlaws like Billy the Kid and Jesse James had been killed. The cowboys saw their lives changed by a more lawful and urban society.

## RAILROADS AND FENCES CHANGE LIFE ON THE RANGE

When Love first came west, the vast open grasslands and good water meant the newly developing cattle industry could grow along with the railroads. Men like Charles Goodnight could fatten their Texas longhorns, hire young cowboys to drive them to the cattle towns to be shipped east or sold to the U.S. Cavalry, and make a huge profit off their sale. The long cattle drives ended in towns like Dodge City, Abilene, Ellsworth, or Cheyenne where the cattle were sold and loaded on trains to the slaughterhouses in Chicago or St. Louis. Sometimes Love and the other cowboys delivered their herds to northern ranches in Wyoming, the Dakotas, or the Great Plains states. But barbed wire had been invented and patented by Joseph F. Glidden in 1873, and by 1890, fences held cattle within the confines of the cattle ranches, which stretched for thousands of acres across the western states and the Great Plains. Ranchers in these areas began to raise more herds on their lands as the buffalo disappeared, and cowboys became ordinary wage earners, working around the ranch.

## OFF TO LIVE IN DENVER

Love no longer felt the cowboy life was right for him. As he wrote in his autobiography: "To us wild cowboys of the range used to the wild unrestricted life of the boundless plains, the new order of things did not appeal." In 1889, he gave up being a cowboy and set off to live in Denver, deciding to try something new.

The Denver he found was a big city with wide streets down which horse-drawn buggies rolled and electric trolleys clanged along the tracks. Telephone and telegraph poles lined the streets, and storefronts—sometimes three stories tall—advertised their wares: "Tailoring, Cleaning & Repairs," "Fabric and Notions," or "Dry Goods Store." Church spires stretched to the sky and the new Capital Dome was visible several blocks away. Fancy hotels and Victorian-style brickhouses with green lawns showed that here was a city where rich men had been created by new industries and gambling or the gold and silver discovered in the hills. The city came right up to the Rocky Mountains and on its outskirts farms provided all kinds of food crops. Dozens of railroad cars steamed in and out of Union Station daily, for Denver was the hub of the Rocky Mountain railroads and known as the "Queen of the Plains."

Here, too, Love saw immigrants from Germany, Russia, Italy, Ireland, China, and Japan, and Jews from many European countries. The black population was small, but just as on the Western frontier, African Americans were usually treated a little more kindly. They were seen to be culturally more acceptable than the Chinese, Japanese, Mexicans, and Native Americans. As historian William M. King said in *The Journal of Negro History*: "Whites viewed blacks as superior to the Chinese and American Indians who were believed to be heathens or savages because of the strange languages and unfamiliar cultures."

In Denver, Love met black women who were in great demand for their skills. It was here that Love wed Alice. He never told her last name or how he met her, but she was the second great passion of his life. He and Alice were married August 22, 1889, and they settled down in a rented cottage to start their life together.

Finding work proved difficult for Love, for he had never received a formal education, so many professions were closed to him. Even though he could read and write well he had no formal degree so only manual labor jobs were available to him. As a cowboy, he had used his strength, but there had been challenges and variety in the work as well. A job as a domestic servant would never suit Love, for he needed some excitement and more personal satisfaction. After talking with other African Americans in his neighborhood, he decided he would try railroading as a porter on the Pullman luxury trains. Then, once again, he could see new places and travel the wide open country.

## A PULLMAN PORTER

By the time Love decided to seek a job as a porter, George Pullman, head of the company, had already developed the idea of passengers

At its peak, the Pullman Company was the largest employer of African Americans. Work as a Pullman porter was the first job Nat Love (*above*) had after his cowboy career came to an end.

traveling in luxury on overnight trains. As early as 1863, his idea of pampering travelers had led him to hire ex-slaves who knew how to serve the needs of others. Later, any African-American man who was willing to work long hours for small wages, do the bidding of the passengers, never complain, and always have a ready smile could be hired. The jobs of conductor or engineer were not open to blacks, but in the 1870s and 1880s, most African-American men were happy to have a regular job with regular wages. Pullman porters were looked upon with high regard in their community.

In *The Life and Adventures of Nat Love*, Love recalled the day he went into the Denver office of the Pullman Company. Superintendent Rummels interviewed him right away, inquiring about what Love had done in the past. Love explained that he had been a cowboy since his teenage years. Next, Superintendent Rummels wanted to know if Love knew anyone in Denver who could write him a letter of recommendation and if he could afford the $22 for a porter's uniform. Love replied that he had more than enough money in the bank to purchase a uniform. Well then, the superintendent agreed, with a letter from Mr. Sprangler, Love's banker, he would hire Love for $15 per month. Love could not help but notice that this was half of what he had received for his first job as a cowboy 20 years earlier.

Love set out to the bank to get a recommendation and money for a uniform. The next day when he returned to Superintendent Rummels' office with his letter, Love was told he could start the following day. Like all Pullman porters Love received a rulebook that explained his duties. The rules told how porters were responsible for greeting travelers with "Good morning" or "Good afternoon," and carrying their luggage. Porters made up the berths (beds) at night, served food and beverages, delivered newspapers, and shined shoes. (It was the porter's duty to buy the shoe polish with his own funds.) Should a passenger take an ashtray, towel, or blanket as a souvenir, or if such items appeared missing, the porter must pay to replace them. The porter could take three hours sleep the first night out and none on the second and third. Most important, the porter must always greet passengers with a smile and answer requests promptly.

Love's uniform was not ready so, in a borrowed uniform, Love went down to Union Station a few hours before the train was due to depart. He worked with a longtime porter who showed him how to make up his car and prepare it for the arrival of the travelers. In addition, Love learned all of the chores he was required to do. Love was on the platform in time to carry the bags of each passenger riding in his car. On his first day on the job and with his best smile, Love worked hard to put away the suitcases of his first passengers: a sour-looking spinster from New York, a rather portly red-faced man, and a tall, slim westerner. He then returned to the platform to greet his other incoming passengers. He could not help but feel how different his new job was from that of herding cattle on "the back of a Texas mustang."

As the journey proceeded, Love found it difficult to please his passengers. His biggest blunder occurred after polishing the shoes of his passengers while they slept. He placed the shoes of the westerner by the berth of the spinster and her shoes by that of the red-faced man. All three were quite angry, and when the train reached Salida, Colorado, most of the passengers refused to give Love any tip. He was frustrated for he knew that without tips his meager wages would not be enough to support his family. As Love explained in his book, "On returning to Denver, I again called on Superintendent Rummels and told him I had had enough of the Pullman service."

The superintendent tried to convince Love that he would improve, but Love decided he could find more suitable work elsewhere. He decided to buy a horse and wagon, and from it he sold fruit, vegetables, honey, and chickens around town. For Love it proved a profitable business, and he made a good living until money grew scarce in Denver. By 1893, a depression had spread across the country and people everywhere lost jobs. Love decided he needed a secure income, no matter how small, and again returned to the railroad. This time he was determined to find a way to please his passengers in order to earn all the tips he could. His family was growing, for he now had a daughter as well as a wife.

This time working as a porter, Love not only carried passengers' bags and made up their berths, but he also minded children, took all complaints with a smile and an apology, and even nursed the sick in his car. He soon found which travelers gave the best tips, but he tried to please even those who had few resources. Love also discovered that Pullman spies traveled in disguise in his cars to inform the superintendent of all that happened on his trips. When he was "travelin' the rails," Love would stay in dormitories called porter houses located in the train stations. Like in the cowboy's bunkhouses, the men talked and told stories, and some even spoke disparagingly of their poor wages and long, hard hours. Still, the porters were more frightened of losing their jobs than of suffering poor working conditions. Men who spoke against the company or who talked of forming a union were dismissed for insubordination. The Pullman spies seemed to find out everything. Love wanted to please the management and keep his steady work, and so he had only praise for George Pullman and the company.

White workers also were treated unfairly by the Pullman Company, and in 1894, they formed a union, called the American Railroad Union (ARU), under Eugene V. Debs. African Americans, however, were not allowed to join. Love continued to make his passengers and the management happy and was given the more desirable routes where the passengers proved to be the biggest tippers. His job was secure and he could count on a living wage with the tips he received.

Those African Americans who had been born into freedom were not content to stand by and take whatever Pullman handed them. By the end of the nineteenth century, a new generation of African Americans who had high school or college educations began to take summer jobs as porters. They wanted fair wages and, like W.E.B. Du Bois, looked at their place in America differently from people who had been born slaves. Yet, as Love once said about his service as a porter, "I early recognized the fact that if I expected to succeed in the Pullman service I must make all the friends I could on my runs. We must necessarily be good judges of human nature to be able to please the majority of the people who travel under our care."

After five years, Love received a stripe on his uniform for good service. He traveled the railroad lines from the East Coast to the West Coast and even down into the South. Several times he returned to the Southwest by working on the Santa Fe Train lines, and once again he saw cactus in the spring with their bright orange,

## Brotherhood of Sleeping Car Porters

When George Pullman began hiring ex-slaves to work on his luxury rail-road cars in 1863, his porters gave him loyal service. But by the beginning of the twentieth century many of the African-American porters grew tired of the long hours, low pay, and unfair work rules. The Transportation Act passed by Congress in 1920 gave Pullman employees the right to "collective bargaining," meaning they could try to set better work conditions. The Pullman Company, though, refused any change. Pullman had spies even among the African-American porters, and fired any man who spoke of forming a union for being disloyal to the company.

Nonetheless, more than 500 African American porters formed the Brotherhood of Sleeping Car Porters on August 25, 1925. Some of the leaders among the union organizers had been fired from their jobs, so the men decided it would be wise to find a leader who was not a Pullman porter. The men asked A. Phillip Randolph, an African-American leader who had helped start several political and trade unions, to lead them. Many of the porters who feared losing their jobs, refused to support the union. Other men believed that porters deserved a decent living wage and supported the Brotherhood, but they did so in secret. Some of these men sent their wives to meetings and paid money in secret to support the union. The Pullman Company opposed the union through firings, dirty deeds, court procedures, and propaganda, but the Brotherhood persisted in its struggle for justice. Over the long years spent trying to gain acceptance for their union, the Brotherhood developed a system of counterspies to combat the dirty trick practices of the Pullman Company. Finally, on August 25, 1937, the Supreme Court ruled in the union's favor. It was a day to remember: The Pullman Company, a major U.S. corporation, agreed to a labor contract with the first all-African-American union—The Brotherhood of Sleeping Car Porters.

pink, and yellow blooms. He traveled to New York City and even up to see Niagara Falls, between New York State and Toronto, Canada. He worked through the snow-capped Rocky Mountains and along

Love was proud of the work he did for the Pullman Company and did not wish to antagonize his supervisors, despite having had to endure insults and racial epithets. Here, Love is pictured (*far left*) with his coworkers at the end of his career.

the Pacific Ocean into San Pedro and Los Angeles. After five more years, he received another stripe and soon after, he transferred to the San Pedro, Los Angeles, & Salt Lake Railroad (S.P., L.A., & S.L.).

By the early 1900s, some of the Pullman cars were just sitting coaches, but Love still dusted off a traveler's coat as he or she left his car. He once recalled a time when he went to dust off a man, the man handed him two pennies and tried to insult him, saying, "Some porters needed calling down and some needed knocking." Whereupon Love smiled, picked up the man's satchel and boxes, took them outside and set them on the platform. He would not waste his breath with such a man.

# STILL SEEKING THE DREAM

All his adult life, Love had been determined to be judged by his accomplishments and not by the color of his skin. He longed to escape racial prejudice and segregation. As a porter, he continued to earn superior ratings on the job. When he traveled the West Coast route on the San Pedro, Los Angeles, & Salt Lake line, he noticed a small, but thriving community of African Americans living in Los Angeles. He discovered that the city had integrated public schools, nonsegregated housing, jobs, political groups, and access to a legal system that treated African Americans fairly. It was a place where African-American males voted in public elections. (Women— whether white or black—did not receive the right to vote until 1920.) During the same years in the South, where Love had been born, violence was commonplace, and the Ku Klux Klan (KKK) terrorized and killed African Americans who stood up for their rights. Between 1882 and 1901, more than 2,000 African-American men were hanged and lynched. Most lynchings happened in rural areas, but mob violence against blacks happened all over.

The Los Angeles African-American community offered Love and his family the possibility of a middle-class lifestyle with cultural organizations and black newspapers. One African-American newspaper, the *Liberator,* printed glowing reports of the possibilities for blacks in California. As its editor, former slave Jefferson Lewis Edmonds, wrote in the paper in 1911:

> Only a few years ago, the bulk of our present colored populations came here from the South without any money, in search of better things and were not disappointed. The hospitable white people received them kindly, employed them at good wages, treated them as men and women, furnished their children with the best educational advantages offered anywhere…. They were treated absolutely fair in courts…. Feeling perfectly safe, the colored people planted themselves [here]. All the Negro wants is an opportunity to develop himself.

The African-American population in Los Angeles increased from 2,131 in 1900 to 7,599 in 1910 to 15,579 in 1920, making it the largest and fastest growing black population in the West. Love must have been impressed by the wonders of life for an African American in Los Angeles. He found the land beautiful with its orange groves, sandy beaches, sunny climate, and foamy ocean waves. So once again he chose to live in a place where he could have a lifestyle that was similar to that of white citizens, and he moved with his wife and almost grown-up daughter to Los Angeles.

## REMEMBERING OLD TIMES

While working on the S.P., L.A., & S. L. line, Love ran into friends from his old cowboy years. One day he came across Billy Blood, now known as Conductor William H. Blood. He and Billy reminisced about their time on the range. Often he saw E. W. Gillett, a general passenger agent, whom he had first known during his cowboy life. Remembering those days and seeing old friends started Love thinking about writing his autobiography. A new century was beginning, and he realized that the cowboys of the Old West had become American heroes. Buffalo Bill Cody, Wild Bill Hickock, and Calamity Jane—all people he remembered from his cowboy days—traveled and performed in the "Wild West Show." With its depictions of frontier life, the performances drew large audiences interested in the Old West.

Love had read dime-store Westerns, and he had even found magazines like the *Wild West Weekly*, which, as its banner said, told "stories and sketches of the Western Life." Calamity Jane had published her short autobiography, *The Life and Adventures of Calamity Jane*, in 1896. Besides this book, Love had read the autobiographies of ex-slaves like Frederick Douglass and Booker T. Washington, books that had sold many copies. Ambitious as he was, Love thought, why wouldn't his autobiography—which would tell of life both as a slave and as a cowboy—be popular as well? In his spare time, Love worked on his story.

Love continued serving as a Pullman porter, and after 15 years, he earned a third stripe on his sleeve for good service. Still, he grew tired of being away from home so often, and he took a job as a courier with General Securities Company in Los Angeles where he delivered important documents around the city. With more time at home, he finished his book and soon found a publisher. Love decided to title it *The Life and Adventures of Nat Love Better Known in the Cattle Country as "Deadwood Dick."* The subtitle claimed "A True History of Slavery Days, Life on the Great Cattle Ranges and on the Plains of the 'Wild and Woolly' West, Based on Facts, and Personal Experiences of the Author."

Before it was published, Love took his family down to the photo studio where he posed in his best suit alongside his fashionably dressed wife and daughter. He felt it was important to show the success he had achieved despite his humble beginnings. Then he was photographed in his Pullman porter's uniform, in his General Securities uniform, and as a cowpuncher with chaps, gun belt, rifle, and a lariat and saddle. This photo he titled "In My Fighting Clothes," for all the photographs would be printed in his book. In addition to the photographs, Love included sketches by S. Campbell of his adventures as a slave boy and as a cowboy. He described his escapades in the South and in the West using the same narrative style

Nat Love is pictured with his wife, Alice, and their daughter in their finest clothes to be printed in his autobiography. Love wanted to show how much he had achieved despite his beginnings as a slave.

as the popular Western dime novels. For some explanations of his early years, he copied the style of the slave narratives of Douglass and Washington. Although he had dedicated the book to his wife, he paid homage to "my mother's Sainted name."

Love's book was published in 1907 by Way Side Press, and to his delight, it sold many copies and became widely successful. With his entrepreneurial skills, he had made money off his book, so he moved his family to Santa Monica and bought a home nearer to the sea.

## A LIFE WELL LIVED

In 1914, life in Los Angeles changed. For one thing, fighting broke out in Europe, shocking most Americans as World War I began. Closer to home in Los Angeles, blacks bitterly opposed the Shenk Rule, enacted by city attorney John Shenk, which allowed public places to charge higher prices to black customers than to whites. By then, Love was 60 years old and had already triumphed over the racial prejudice he had met in Tennessee. All his life he had faced challenges with a zeal that others seemed to lack. When the United States entered World War I in 1917, he was too old to serve, but younger African Americans served in segregated units in the military. The war brought shortages of food and goods to the nation, but that, too, Love had faced before.

Before his death in 1921 at age 67, Love could look back proudly on a life that had brought him far from his early days as a slave. The successes he had achieved through his skills and hard work brought him great satisfaction. Despite entering the world as a poor slave and never receiving a formal education, he had been able, he said in his autobiography, "[to] enjoy the trust and confidence of my employers and the homage of the men many of whom were indebted to me on occasions when my long rope or ever ready [.45 Colt] pistol had saved them from serious injury or death."

In a time of great racial prejudice, Nat Love had gained respect from both Anglos and African Americans. His parents had instilled in him a confidence and pride that allowed his independent spirit to thrive. Although he had to leave his birthplace and his family to achieve all he did, he created for himself a life of dignity as well as adventure at a time when most African Americans had little hope of finding success.

# CHRONOLOGY

**1854**    Nat Love is born on a slave plantation in Tennessee.

**1860**    Abraham Lincoln is elected president of the United States.

**1861**    Civil War begins at Fort Sumter in Charleston Harbor, South Carolina.

**1863**    President Lincoln issues Emancipation Proclamation.

African-American soldiers enter Union army; freedmen number 52,000 troops and ex-slaves number more than 134,000.

Entrepreneur George Pullman builds a luxury railroad car and begins the Pullman Palace Car Company.

**1865**    **April 9**    General Robert E. Lee surrenders at Appomattox Court House in Virginia to General Ulysses S. Grant, and the Civil War ends.

**April 14**    President Lincoln is shot and killed at the Ford Theatre in Washington, D.C. Thirteenth Amendment to the U.S. Constitution is ratified.

Love's family becomes free and begins life as tenant farmers in Tennessee.

**1867**   Nat Love's father dies; leaves Nat and his brother Jordan to work the land.

**1868**   The Fourteenth Amendment to the U.S. Constitution is ratified. Love gets his first paid job.

**1869**   Love leaves home and heads to Kansas to find a better life in the West; he gets hired as a cow-boy with the Duval Outfit from the Texas Panhandle. Love first encounters Native Americans.

**May 10**   Union Pacific and the Central Pacific railroad lines join San Francisco to Chicago by meeting in Promontory Point, Utah.

# TIMELINE

1861–1865: American Civil War is fought. At war's end, Love's family becomes free; begins life as tenant farmers in Tennessee

1876: Named Deadwood Dick for his championship skills in cowboy contest

**1854**

**1877**

1854: Nat Love born on slave plantation in Tennessee

1869: Love heads to Kansas to find a better life in the West; hired as a cowboy with the Duval Outfit from the Texas Panhandle; has first encounter with Native Americans

1877: Gets lost in a snowstorm, but is found and saved by his crew

**1870** Fifteenth Amendment to the U.S. Constitution is ratified; Love learns to be a cowboy.

**1872** Love joins the Gallinger outfit near the Gila River in Arizona Territory. Soon afterward he becomes a brand reader for the outfit.

**1873** Joseph F. Glidden invents barbed wire on his farm in DeKalb, Illinois, making it possible to pen in cattle.

**1876** June 22 Battle of the Little Big Horn; Colonel George A. Custer attacks Native American vil-lage along the Little Big Horn River in Montana; Custer and all his men die in the battle against the Cheyenne and Lakota people.

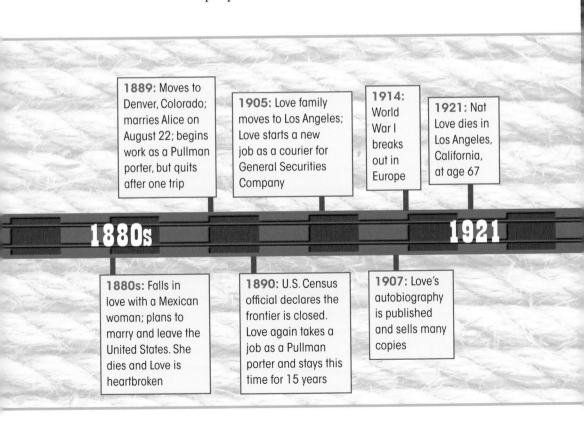

1889: Moves to Denver, Colorado; marries Alice on August 22; begins work as a Pullman porter, but quits after one trip

1905: Love family moves to Los Angeles; Love starts a new job as a courier for General Securities Company

1914: World War I breaks out in Europe

1921: Nat Love dies in Los Angeles, California, at age 67

**1880s**

**1921**

1880s: Falls in love with a Mexican woman; plans to marry and leave the United States. She dies and Love is heartbroken

1890: U.S. Census official declares the frontier is closed. Love again takes a job as a Pullman porter and stays this time for 15 years

1907: Love's autobiography is published and sells many copies

**July 4**    Love is given the name Deadwood Dick for his championship skills in a cowboy contest in Deadwood, South Dakota.

**1877**    Southern states return to home rule and continue oppression against African-American rights.

Love gets lost in a snowstorm but is rescued by his crew.

**1878**    On a cattle drive to Junction City, Kansas, horses stampede; Love saves a fellow crew member while crossing the Wakeney River.

**1880s**    Love falls in love with a Mexican woman and plans to marry and leave the United States; she dies, and Love is heartbroken.

**1889**    Love finds the cowboy life no longer right for him.

**August 22**    Love moves to Denver, Colorado, and marries Alice. He begins work as a Pullman porter but quits after one trip.

**1890**    U.S. Census official declares the frontier is closed. Love again takes a job as a Pullman porter and stays this time for 15 years.

**1893–1897**    General business depression spreads across the United States.

**1894**    American Railroad Union (ARU) is formed with Eugene V. Debs as president; ARU workers strike against Pullman Car Company.

**1905**    The Love family moves to Los Angeles; Love starts a new job as a courier for General Securities Company.

**1907**    Love's autobiography is published and sells many copies.

**1909**  The National Association for the Advancement of Colored People (NAACP) is founded with the help of W.E.B. Du Bois.

**1912**  New Mexico Territory and Arizona Territory gain statehood.

**1914**  The First World War begins in Europe.

**1917**  The United States enters the First World War.

**1918**  An armistice ends the First World War.

**1921**  Nat Love dies in Los Angeles, California, at age 67.

# GLOSSARY

**abolitionist**  A person who wants to abolish or terminate slavery.

**amendments to the U.S. Constitution**

> **Thirteenth Amendment**  adopted in 1865, outlawed slavery in the United States

> **Fourteenth Amendment**  adopted in 1868, granted civil rights and equal protection of the law to male citizens.

> **Fifteenth Amendment**  adopted in 1870, said the right to vote could not be denied because of "race, color or previous conditions of servitude (slavery)."

**Anglo**  Usually meaning a person from England or of European descent.

**antimiscegenation laws**  Outlawed marriage between white and nonwhite persons.

**autobiography**  The story of a person's life written by that person.

**barbed wire**  Twisted strands of fence wire with barbs at regular intervals. The sharp barbs keep animals away.

**bronco**  A wild or semi-wild horse of western North America.

**buffalo chips**  Dried buffalo dung, which was used to make campfires when wood was unavailable.

**cash crop**  Crops grown to provide cash to the grower instead of food to feed the family.

**cattle barons** Ranchers from Arizona and Texas to Montana, Colorado, and Wyoming who used open land to graze their cattle and grew rich selling them in the years after the Civil War.

**cattle drive** A long trip herding cattle over harsh terrain along trails leading to cattle towns; a trip of 1,200 miles (1,931 km) took cowboys about four months.

**cattle rustler** A person who steals cattle.

**cattle town** The end of the trail where buyers from the East purchased the livestock and put it on railroad cars headed for Chicago or New York. These included towns in Kansas like Dodge City, Wichita, Ellsworth, and Abilene, and Kansas City, Missouri.

**chaps** A type of legging fitted over the jeans to protect the cowboys' legs as they ride through rough country against both the horse and cacti or thorny chaparral (shrubs).

**chattel** A type of moveable property, such as a cow or horse; in the antebellum South, slaves were considered valuable property, or chattel.

**chuck wagon** A farm wagon that had been built as a moving kitchen stocked with food and medicine for the crew. Driven by the cook, it usually went ahead to a pre-decided camping ground and waited for the cowboys and herd to arrive.

**civil rights** Rights belonging to a person by virtue of his or her status as a citizen. The first ten amendments to the U.S. Constitution as well as the Thirteenth, Fourteenth, and Fifteenth amendments are usually considered civil rights.

**civil rights movement** An effort by African Americans and white activists, the National Association for the Advancement of Colored People (NAACP), and others to bring racial equality to the nation. As early as the 1930s, the Legal Defense Fund of the NAACP began an assault on the judicial system to outlaw segregation, but from the 1950s to the 1970s and beyond, activists brought increased pressure to provide civil rights to all people.

**Civil War**   The bloodiest war in American history officially began when Fort Sumter in Charleston Harbor in South Carolina was attacked by Confederate troops on April 12, 1861.

**colored people or Negroes**   In the nineteenth and early twentieth centuries, African Americans were generally called colored people or Negroes.

**Confederate states**   Slave-holding states that seceded from the United States as a result of Abraham Lincoln's election and his decision not to compromise on the extension of slavery.

**cowpuncher**   Known in some parts of the country as cowhand or buckaroo, all the men were called cowboys.

**dime-novel Westerns**   Popular and inexpensive novels of the adventures of white male cowboys written at the end of the nineteenth century and the beginning of the twentieth.

**drag riders**   One or two crew members who rode behind the herd and kept the stragglers moving forward. It was a dusty place to ride, so they were also known as dust eaters.

**drover**   A trail boss who made all the important the decisions about how fast to travel, how to avoid hazards, when to stop and where. Sometimes he owned the herd.

**ex-slave**   Those African Americans that had once been held in bondage.

**flank riders**   The cowboys who rode at the sides of the herd, some near the lead cattle to keep them going in the right direction; others rode up and down the sides of the herd to keep the cattle from straying too far from the trail.

**freedmen**   African Americans who had been born free or who had been freed by proclamation or amendment. They often had restricted rights, especially in the South, but could buy and own property.

**grazing wars**   Sheep herders, cattlemen, and settlers grazing their livestock on public lands often used weapons instead of the courts to decide who had rights to the open lands and water holes.

**Great Plains**   The wide area between the Mississippi River and the Rocky Mountains, which could support livestock and grain crops such as wheat.

**greenhorn**   Originally a young animal with immature horns, cowboys often called an inexperienced crew member a greenhorn until he learned his trade.

**Homestead Act 1862**   Offered free or cheap land to people who would settle in the West and improve the property.

**Jim Crow laws**   A Supreme Court ruling in 1883 struck down the Civil Rights Act of 1875, which prohibited segregated public facilities, such as hospitals, streetcars, and parks. From then on, laws written by Southern states to enforce segregation became known as Jim Crow laws. These laws set up systems designed to keep African Americans separated from white citizens in the South.

**Ku Klux Klan (KKK)**   The white supremacist terrorist organization first formed by Civil War veterans in Tennessee in 1866. It spread quickly in the South and used harassment, beatings, lynching, and murder to try to keep African Americans from gaining their rights as citizens.

**lariat**   A rope with a running noose; a lasso.

***The Liberator***   The original abolitionist newspaper published by William Lloyd Garrison beginning in 1831 until the end of the Civil War; it described the evils of slavery. The Los Angeles *Liberator* was published by Joseph Lewis Edmonds, an ex-slave who arrived in the city in 1896. In 1900, he began a monthly newspaper for the African-American community.

**maverick**   An unbranded range animal, especially a calf.

**mustang**   A wild horse of the western plains.

**National Association for the Advancement of Colored People (NAACP)**   Formed in 1909 by W.E.B. Du Bois and others to gain voting rights for African Americans and to end inequality and racial segregation in public facilities, including schools.

**peculiar institution**    Because slave labor provided big profits for many in the South, Southerners developed social attitudes that justified the use of slaves. Using arguments that the Bible referred to slavery, a weaker race needed to be guided, or it was the natural order of things that some should dominate others, slave labor became a way of life. It was in practice a form of extreme and deep-felt racism.

**Ph.D.**    The most advanced degree a university offers; W.E.B. Du Bois was the first African American to receive this advanced degree from Harvard University.

**porter house**    A dormitory, usually in the railroad station, where porters could stay while waiting for their next trip.

**quirt**    A riding whip with a short handle and a lash of rawhide.

**railhead**    A town that had railroad access.

**Reconstruction Period**    The period from 1865 to 1877 during which the Confederate states were forced to change political and social practices before they could be fully readmitted into the Union. After readmission, they reversed many practices and made segregation common policy.

**remuda**    From the Spanish *remudar,* to exchange. Each morning, extra horses were brought to the camping grounds so the cowboys could choose a fresh horse for the day's ride. Most cowboys had favorite horses, though all the horses belonged to the outfit's owner.

**run**    A certain section or distance on various railroad lines, such as between Salt Lake City and Los Angeles.

**sharecropper**    A farmer who gives a share of his crop to the landlord as a rent payment for using the land.

**slave narrative**   An account, usually an autobiography, written by an ex-slave about life in bondage.

**stampede**   A sudden, headlong rush of startled animals; the cause of many cowboys' death as they were trampled under the hooves of the cattle.

**tenant farmer**   A farmer who rents or uses land owned by another person.

**union**   An association of wage earners organized to gain fair wages and working conditions from their employer.

**vaqueros**   Mexican cowboys who during a period of 300 years developed the dress and techniques used by cowboys in the United States.

**Wild West**   Both the reality and myths grew about life on the American frontier from the 1840s to the 1890s. Ranchers, miners, trappers, American Indians, cowboys, outlaws, U.S. marshals, frontier towns, and military forts all played a part in the history and legends that developed in the West.

**wrangler**   The lowest status of a cowboy crew; he was responsible for the crew's horses. Because each cowboy rode several horses, the wrangler herded from 20 to 100 horses.

# BIBLIOGRAPHY

Allmendinger, Blake. *The Cowboy Representations of Labor in an American Work Culture*. New York: Oxford University Press, 1992.

Costanzo, Angelo. "Review: The Life and Adventures of Nat Love by Nat Love." *MELUS*, 22, no. 3 (Autumn 1997): 218–220.

De Graaf, Lawrence B., Kevin Mulroy, and Quintard Taylor, eds. *Seeking El Dorado: African Americans in California*. Los Angeles: Autry Museum of Western Heritage, 2001.

Douglass, Frederick. *Narrative of the Life of Frederick Douglass: An American Slave Written By Himself*. Boston: Harvard University Press, 1991.

Du Bois, W.E.B. *The Soul of Black Folks*. New York: Fine Creative Media, Inc., 2003.

Durham, Philip, and Everett L. Jones. *The Negro Cowboys*. New York: Dodd, Mead & Company, 1965.

Forbis, William F. *The Old West: The Cowboy*. New York: Time-Life Books, 1973.

Frantz, Joe Bertrand, and Julian Ernest Choate. *The American Cowboy: The Myth and the Reality*. Norman: University of Oklahoma Press, 1955.

Gard, Wayne. *The Chisholm Trail*. Norman: University of Oklahoma Press, 1979.

Gates, Henry, Jr., ed. *The Classic Slave Narratives*. New York: New American Library, 1987.

Hardaway, Roger, D. "The African American Cowboys on the Western Frontier." *Negro History Bulletin* (January-December) 2001: 27–32.

Johnson, Willard B. "Tracing Trails of Blood on Ice: Commemorating 'The Great Escape' in 1861–1862 of Indians and Blacks into Kansas." *Negro History Bulletin* (January-December 2001): 1–10.

Katz, William Loren. *The Black West*, 3rd ed. Seattle: Open Hand Publishing, Inc., 1987.

Love, Nat. *The Life and Adventures of Nat Love*. The American Negro History and Literary Series. William Loren Katz, ed. New York: Arno Press, Inc., 1968.

McKissack, Patricia, and Frederick McKissack. *A Long Hard Journey: The Story of the Pullman Porters*. New York: Walker & Company, 1989.

Moore, Jesse T. "Seeking a New Life: Blacks in a Post-Civil War Culture." *Journal of Negro History*, 78 (1993): 166–186.

Norton, Mary Beth, David F. Katzman, David W. Bright, Howard P. Chudacoff, Thomas G. Patterson, William M. Tuttle, and Paul D. Escott. *A People and a Nation: A History of the United States*. 6th ed. New York: Houghton Mifflin Company, 2001.

Painter, Nell Irvin. *Exodusters*. New York: Knopf, 1976.

Peavy, Linda, and Ursula Smith. *Pioneer Women: The Lives of Women on the Frontier*. Norman: University of Oklahoma Press, 1996.

Porter, Kenneth Wiggins. *The Negro on the American Frontier*. New York: Arno Press and *The New York Times*, 1971.

———. "Negro Labor in the Western Cattle Industry 1869–1900." *Labor History*, 10, no. 3 (summer 1969): 346–374.

Santino, Jack. *Miles of Smiles, Years of Struggle: Stories of Black Pullman Porters*. Chicago: University of Illinois Press, 1989.

Savage, W. Sherman. *Blacks in the West*. Westport: Greenwood Press, 1976.

Scheckel, Susan. "Home on the Train: Race and Mobility in the Life of Nat Love." *American Literature*, 74, no.2 (June 2002): 219–250.

Schneirov, Richard, Shelton Stromquist, and Nick Salvatore. *The Pullman Strike and the Crisis of the 1890s.* Chicago: University of Chicago Press, 1999.

Speirs, Kenneth. "Writing Self (Effacingly): E-Raced-D Perspectives in the Life and Adventures of Nat Love." *Western American Literature,* 70, no. 3 (Fall 2005): 301–320.

Washington, Booker T. *Up From Slavery.* Edited by W. Fitzhugh Brundage. Boston: Bedford/St. Martins Press, 2003.

Young, Paul E. *Back Trail of an Old Cowboy.* Lincoln: University of Nebraska Press, 1983.

# FURTHER RESOURCES

Freedman, Russell. *In the Days of the Vaqueros.* New York: Clairon Books, 2001.

———. *Cowboys of the Wild West.* New York: Clairon Books, 1985.

George, Charles. *Life Under the Jim Crow Laws.* San Diego, Calif.: Lucent Books, 2000.

McPherson, James M. *Into the West.* New York: Atheneum, 2006.

Miller, William. *Frederick Douglass: The Last Days of Slavery.* New York: Lee & Low Books, 1995.

Sanford, William R. *The Chisholm Trail.* Berkeley Heights: Enslow Publishing, Inc., 2000.

Stewart, Gail B. *Cowboys in the Old West.* San Diego, Calif.: Lucent Books, 1995.

Weidt, Maryann N. *Voice of Freedom: A Story About Frederick Douglass.* Minneapolis: Lerner Publications, 2001.

Waltrip, Lela, and Rufus Waltrip. *Cowboys and Cattlemen.* New York: David McKay Company, Inc., 1967.

## Web Sites

### African American History and Culture
*http://www.indianahumanities.org/htgAF.htm*
This Web site has detailed information relating to African-American history, people of interest, and references to materials in various media.

### African American Library
*www.academicinfo.net/africanamlibrary.html*

This site is an online reference center that provides free, independent, and accurate information for researchers and students.

**Black American West Museum**

*www.blackamericanwestmuseum.com*

Online source for learning the history of buffalo soldiers, miners, pioneers, early explorers, cowboys, and homesteaders in the American West.

**Black Cowboys**

*www.blackcowboys.com*

A Web site for information about black cowboys. Includes biographies of famous cowboys and links to other sites on the subject.

**Buffalo Soldiers and Indian Wars**

*http://www.buffalosoldier.net/*

This Web site is dedicated to providing information about black soldiers, called buffalo soldiers, who fought in American wars with and against American Indians.

**Denver History**

*http://www.denvergov.org/aboutdenver/history_narrative.asp*

This site is dedicated to the history of Denver, Colorado, from its founding to today.

**Legends of America**

*http://www.legendsofamerica.com/WE-NatLove1.html*

A travel site for those interested in the American frontier. Includes a biography of Love and photographs from the Old West.

**Nat Love**

*www.nat-love.com*

All you need to know about cowboy Nat Love, including an excerpt from his autobiography *The Life and Adventures of Nat Love, Better Known in the Cattle Country as "Deadwood Dick."*

**PBS: African American World**

*www.pbs.org/wnet/aaworld/reference/books.html*

A library of books, films, and other resources for "expanding your knowledge of African-American history and culture."

**The Traveling History Trunk**

*http://swco.ttu.edu/history_trunk/trunkindex.html*

Assembled materials used by educators for teaching students about the ranching life in Texas. Includes the Ranching Frontier Glossary, photographs, slide shows, suggested activities, quizzes, recipes, and links to other sources.

# PICTURE CREDITS

## Page

# INDEX

# ABOUT THE AUTHOR

Barbara Lee Bloom grew up in California and received her undergraduate degree in history from the University of California, Los Angeles. She received a doctorate from the University of Vermont. She is an emeritus professor of history at Champlain College in Vermont. Her biographies for young people have been published in the United States and abroad. Other books for young people include *The Mexican Americans*, *The Chinese Americans*, and *The Organization of American States*.